Getting It

Getting It

❖

Persuading Organizations and Individuals to Be More Comfortable with People with Disabilities

By Melissa Marshall

People with Disabilities Press,
Stanley D. Klein, Ph.D., Series Editor
iUniverse, Inc.
San Jose New York Lincoln Shanghai

Getting It
Persuading Organizations and Individuals to Be More Comfortable with People with Disabilities

People with Disabilities Press,
Stanley D. Klein, Ph.D., Series Editor
iUniverse, Inc.
an imprint of iUniverse, Inc.

For information address:
iUniverse, Inc.
5220 S. 16th St., Suite 200
Lincoln, NE 68512
www.iuniverse.com

Photo by Maria Story

Cover graphic by Anita Cox

ISBN: 0-595-21253-0

Printed in the United States of America

Dedicated to Ken, Nick, Liam and Ruth (my Mom)

Contents

Acknowledgements

Many people and organizations made this book possible. I'd like to thank the Boston Globe Foundation for awarding me a grant to develop, present and evaluate disability awareness training. The Foundation's support provided me the luxury of being able to research and plan as well as hone my training skills. I'd particularly like to thank Foundation staff Suzanne Maas and Klare Shaw for their flexibility and willingness to nurture my creativity. I would like to thank Louise Fisher, Executive Director of Progressive Attitudes, for marketing my trainings to corporations and enabling me to train in an entirely new arena.

I would also like to thank the Connecticut Council on Developmental Disability for awarding me funding to provide training in city high schools. Special thanks to the administration, teachers, staff and students of Weaver High School for being gracious hosts and allowing me enormous access to the student body. I'd like to thank Chris Palames of Independent Living Resources for providing me with contacts and allowing me to partake of numerous opportunities to do this work.

I'd also like to thank those who facilitated the writing of this book. Ellanah Sherman worked tirelessly to edit initial drafts; her insight and wit have been invaluable during this process. Liza Steinkamp was responsible for final edits. Kathryn Baptista surreptitiously read the first chapters of the book and gave me the support, encouragement and incentive to keep writing. I'd like to thank Stan Klein of People with Disabilities Press for understanding the value of disability related literature. I'd also like to thank Lisa Blumberg for introducing me to Stan and for bringing rigorous intellectual analysis to the disability rights movement and to disability rights literature.

I'd like to thank my family—my mom for being my first role model of an advocate, my husband Ken for having the utmost faith and confidence in all my endeavors, my son Nick for always being interested in what I do, and especially my son Liam for having the courtesy to occasionally nap while I wrote this book.

1

Getting Started

On July 26, 1990, I was staying at the home of a sick friend. President George Bush, along with 10,000 people with disabilities as witnesses, was in Washington signing the Americans with Disabilities Act—the broadest sweeping civil rights legislation protecting people with disabilities in the history of the planet. I'm tempted to chastise the press for not grasping the significance of the ADA, but it's hard to blame them when even the Congress who enacted the law didn't fully appreciate the impact it could and would have on all Americans. Over a decade later, the ADA continues to literally change the shape of the American landscape. Not only has it changed our built environment, it has begun to change the way that the American public sees people with disabilities, and I think even more importantly, the way we see ourselves.

So what has this got to do with disability diversity training? From my perspective it has everything to do with it. See, prior to the passage of the ADA, I was the executive director of what is called a Center for Independent Living for people with disabilities. Independent living centers were started in the 1970's as an alternative to traditional social work and vocational rehabilitation programs. What makes independent living centers different from traditional social services agencies is that they are run by and for people with disabilities. The underlying premise of independent living centers is that people with disabilities are the experts who best know their wants and needs and should be treated as such. Contrary to what the name implies, no one lives at an independent living center. Rather, centers offer advocacy, information and

1

other support to enable people with disabilities to live as independently as they choose, in most cases in the community. Independent living centers were the building block of the disability rights movement—the civil rights movement that spawned the passage of the ADA.

After the ADA had been signed, I left my more or less secure job at the Center for Independent Living. It was secure in that there was a regular if small weekly paycheck. Paychecks were contingent on the renewal of state and federal grants. Funding often came late and every now and then we had to beg the state legislature not to shut us down. I guess the term "secure" has a different meaning in the wonderful world of non-profits. Anyway, I left the Center to pursue my fortune as a consultant. As a consultant, I would provide training and technical assistance in the ADA and other disability rights law. At least that's what I told people at my going away party.

I was now a trainer. It wasn't like anyone had actually hired me or anything. My friend and colleague, Chris Palames, invited me to come and work for him in his single person non-profit; the only rub was that I would have to generate my own work. I decided not to work with Chris until we had been notified that we had received a major federal grant for which we had applied. Then a friend said, "So, if you don't get the grant are you going to stay where you are forever and never give yourself the opportunity to really learn about the ADA?" She was right. I wouldn't be able to master the law as long as I was also an administrator who had to spend the majority of her time doing icky things like writing grants and supervising people. So, with a loan from my friend Julie, the same person who told me to go already, I was on my way.

Well, I did manage to get work doing ADA training and technical assistance, that is providing people with information that they might need to help them implement the law. My family didn't starve and I managed to pay Julie back. Not only did I get to master the law in a way that wasn't possible in my old position, I got to do one of the things that I like best in life—training. Now are you beginning to see how all this information is relevant?

Providing training in the ADA and other disability rights law is much more than simply explaining legal requirements to someone who has obligations. Even in scripted training where every word that comes out of my mouth has to be pre-approved by some federal agency or by a client (yes, there are clients who hire you to train them and then want to approve what you say ahead of time—don't ask) I try to include more than legal facts.

There are a couple of reasons why I do this. First, legal facts are boring to most people. Just because I find the regulations of Title II of the ADA scintillating reading doesn't mean that I'm not aware of this, as well as of my general need to get a life. People do not learn as well when they are bored. Therefore, as a trainer, it is my job to make this material interesting. Second, most people, including people with disabilities, have some level of discomfort with people with disabilities and disability issues. Just as people don't learn well when they are bored, they don't learn well when they are uncomfortable. Therefore, it is also part of my job to make them more comfortable.

Legal training was only half of the equation. Awareness training was the other half. If any actual social change was to happen there really needed to be both. I saw organizations that sincerely wanted to comply with the law fumble because staff was uncomfortable with disability issues.

I try to breathe life into the law by showing its connection to real people who happen to have disabilities and real organizations that happen to have obligations under disability rights law. I try to make the material fun and interesting by including both lighthearted and serious anecdotes and examples about actual people with disabilities.

As I did more and more training, I came to the realization that I could increase participants' comfort level with people with disabilities and disability issues only so much during the course of a short or even a long legal training. I was already packing in way too much content.

I became enthralled with the idea of having time to solely talk about attitudes toward people with disabilities and maybe even strategizing about ways to change behavior that reflected discomfort around people with disabilities. In the past, I had always called this type of training *disability awareness training.* I now think of it as disability diversity training. This better reflects the complexity and richness of the process.

When I learned that I'd gotten a grant from the Boston Globe Foundation to develop and pilot what I then called disability awareness training, I was ecstatic. This is something that I'd wanted to do since I was six years old and kids teased me about how I walked. I had funding to research and develop a training that would draw from and adapt successful materials from other disability and racial and ethnic diversity trainings. I would have time to think about the process of providing training and develop a coherent model. I decided that I might even throw in a few ideas of my own.

Not having the time or money to develop training never stopped me from doing it. I did my first training series as a junior in high school for a class in human interaction. (Yes, I went to one of those earthy-crunchy alternative high schools that unfortunately died at the end of the seventies as I graduated.) I did a day of disability etiquette: What do you do when you come across a disabled person? I also had my teacher's husband come in and do a slide show. It turns out that he was a social worker at a place in Massachusetts called a hospital school. That's where they sent and still send some kids with disabilities who it is decided don't belong in school. Louie wasn't a traditional social worker—he talked about something called the disability rights movement. It was then that I learned that there were other people who thought that access was a civil right. I'm not sure what the other students got out of it, if anything, but it changed my life.

It was through dumb luck that I presented trainings for the next fifteen years. I was too distracted by the minutia of life, like law school and being the founding director of a non-profit, to put concerted effort into developing training. Typically, I developed training in the car on the way to the event—the longer the commute, the more detailed the planning.

I had resigned from my job as the executive director of a Center for Independent Living to pursue my fortune as a consultant who did training in the Americans with Disabilities Act (ADA), and now as an awareness trainer, I finally had time to think about training. When the excitement faded, I got terrified. What if I didn't really have anything to say about disability? What if the perfect awareness training already existed and I had nothing to add to it? What did I mean by awareness training anyway? Does it work? Would it really change anything or was presenting awareness training just a hideout for burnt out disability rights activists who were tired of confrontation? So much for the thrill of a blank slate...

The blank slate loomed for a while. I was busy with other projects and I needed to let ideas percolate. I didn't even believe myself when I said that I was in the process of developing training, but it turned out to be true. At my undergraduate school, students and faculty talked about a process called creative floundering. This is a term used to describe students who take their time to figure out what they want to do academically and how to do it. Most of the creative flounderers that I knew drowned and that's exactly what I was afraid of doing. Fortunately, my somewhat pathological fear of inertia propelled me through the training development process.

What did I want in a training anyway? For a while the only way I could answer that question was to clarify what I did not want. I did not want to produce a training that encouraged people without disabilities to be condescending to, or worse, inspired by people with disabilities. I did not want a training model that oversimplified the situation of people with disabilities and implied that the major difficulties encountered by people with disabilities is a problem of attitudinal barriers that can be fixed in a two-hour workshop. I did not want to create a training that did not address disability as a political issue.

I was unwilling to develop a training that used simulation, that is non-disabled people pretending to have a disability for part of a day by using a wheelchair, being blindfolded, or plugging their ears, etc. My problem with simulation is that it is simplistic and tends to elicit a negative simplistic response. Take your average person whose means of mobility is walking. Put them in an old borrowed clunker wheelchair in an inaccessible environment without any training and they're probably not going to have a good time. They might come to realize that the built environment is largely inaccessible which would be a useful insight. But they also might come away from the experience thinking, "My God, I'd kill myself if I had to use one of those things all the time." From there it's a short leap to concluding that "those people are sooooo brave."

Training Hint: If people leave a workshop believing that they would choose death over life as a person with a disability or using phrases like "those people," you haven't had a good outcome.

I don't think simulation is always inappropriate. Under certain circumstances and with the right audience it can be effective. For example, simulation might be useful as part of an access curriculum for design students. (Would it be that design and architecture students actually studied access? But that's another book.)

I actually went to relatively few awareness and diversity trainings. Much of what I saw I didn't like. Training exercises either didn't translate well from racial or sexual orientation training, or if they were disability awareness trainings, they included some or all of the characteristics that I've just described as problematic. I also didn't want my training to be overly derivative, meaning ripped off from other trainers. So much for drawing on the material of others.

Okay, so now that I had a list of activities and outcomes that I didn't want in a training, I had to start searching in earnest for things that I did want to include. It looked like I was going to be on my own for better or worse.

I wanted to produce a training that reached people on a deep level, but did not leave them feeling guilty, vulnerable or otherwise maligned. (I'd already done my stint in a human potential group/cult when I was in college.) I wanted people to get it about disability, whatever it was. I also wanted them to have a good time.

To meet my goal, the training needed to extend well beyond disability etiquette, although I would certainly incorporate etiquette into my trainings. After all, it is hard for people to treat you as an equal when they don't know what to call you, where to look, or how to ask you a question. Yet, that is fairly superficial. I wanted to develop a training that delved deeper than exploring stereotypes of and myths about people with disabilities. This could occupy a portion of a training, but wasn't quite substantial enough to carry an entire curriculum. I needed an idea from which I could develop an activity that could become the cornerstone of the training.

One day I was sitting at the kitchen table of my friend, colleague and collaborator, Chris, talking about the training model. I said that it wasn't so much the stereotypes surrounding disability that I wanted to address, but the archetypes that are thrust upon or taken on by people with disabilities. By archetypes, I meant the powerful almost mythic images that Jung talked about. These are images and ideas that resonate with an entire culture on an almost primal level. I thought of the disabled person as victim, as martyr, as hero, as monster. How was I going to communicate this concept to audiences? I couldn't quite picture myself lecturing on Jung as a brief module in a two-hour training to audiences who may or may not have had any post-secondary education. Plus, it disrupted the whole idea of the training being fun for either participants or myself.

I was stymied for a while, but the idea of incorporating archetypes wouldn't go away.

Training Hint: When an idea won't go away it's probably worth pursuing.

I worked on numerous other projects and read a little about archetypes in my spare time.

One day I was reading a book by Joseph Campbell, a scholar who wrote extensively on myths and archetypes. The name of the book was

The Masks of God. I thought about the title of the book and it dawned on me that the way to communicate about archetypes and disability was for the presenter to embody the archetypes while wearing masks.

This idea obviously needed some fleshing out. How would I—possibly the most unartistic person who ever inhabited the planet—acquire masks? There was no time or money with which to hire an artist. Besides, I didn't even know anyone who did that sort of thing. There really, really wasn't money or time to interview, hire and communicate my ideas to an artist. If I was going to use masks, I would have to make them myself. The idea wasn't totally farfetched. Prior to this I had made a plaster cast mask of my face as a group activity. As I thought about it, I remembered that it was the only non-edible thing that I'd made with my hands that I didn't actively hate.

One day, I bravely (sometimes I tell audiences that this is an example of a time when its okay to regard a person with a disability brave) went to the art supply store and, after warning the clerk not to confuse me with someone who knew what she was doing, asked her to help me select supplies for making masks. I left the store with rolls of gauze infused with plaster, tempera paints, and much trepidation.

With the help of my husband, Ken, I made plaster castings of my face. We added gauze to build up sections of the mask and then sanded them. As we brought them outside and sanded them, neighbors in my housing co-op wondered. But then, they always had.

I now had six casts of my face lying on my kitchen table awaiting decoration. I attributed what I saw as archetypal characters to some of the masks as I was making them. I knew that one was the Hero—the disabled person who had "overcome" his disability and needed no accommodation; another was the Saint—the angelic disabled person who was holier than any mortal. Another would be a Monster—the physically and spiritually deformed person who scares us all.

While under quarantine recovering from adult onset chicken pox, I got bored enough to paint the masks. Perhaps it was the fever. They came out stylized and comic book like. People later told me that this was good because it made them easier to see on stage, as if I'd made them this way intentionally. Being the non-artist that I am, this was my only choice. Again, luck worked in my favor.

Now, the question became could I actually use these props as a part of an awareness training without looking totally stupid? Would people get my message at all? Did I really have a message to present?

I dealt with this quandary the same way I deal with most issues in my life. I talked to anyone who would pretend to listen to me. I later realized that this is an important skill for a trainer to have. The conventional wisdom of my friends, colleagues, and a few acquaintances that I met traveling is that I had a BAD IDEA. After all, my artwork could kindly be described as primitive, and aside from being a total ham I had no qualifications as an actor. Besides that, the concept was a bit amorphous; participants probably wouldn't connect with it. It might scare people. In short, I had no right to do it.

They were of course, correct. I couldn't argue. I didn't. I also didn't listen. At my husband's encouragement, I decided to make a fool of myself and indulge this idea that wouldn't go away. So, I wrote some script fragments for the masks and brought them to my first training. I was very curious as to what they would have to say when they were on stage, as it were.

At first only a few participants got the message of the masks. Others, as my friends had predicted, were completely confused and a little frightened. I hung my hopes on the people who appreciated the masks. I decided that if I couldn't make the masks work because I didn't have the skill or talent, probably someone else could. Maybe it would require funding to hire an artist and some actors, but this seemed to be an idea that would work. In the meantime, I would keep bringing them to trainings to see if I got better with practice.

I want to point out that this was uncharacteristic of me. Granted, I'm notoriously stubborn, but I also tend to take negative criticism, hyperbolize it, and then believe it is the gospel truth. For some reason, this was different.

The masks did become the cornerstone of my awareness training. After I got used to presenting them, training participants became more at ease and were typically quite moved by them.

Moral of the story: An idea that won't go away is probably haunting you for a good reason. At least give it some airtime.

Why Awareness Training and What Did I Want to Communicate?

As I was creating the masks, I was busy thinking of other training activities. Before I moved further, I had to take a hard look at exactly why I wanted to do awareness training and what it was that I wanted to communicate to participants.

Why did I want to do awareness training so badly? My knee jerk response is that I wanted to bring about social change. Being an activist, that's my knee jerk rationalization for many of the things that I "wanna do." Okay, so we all know that I want to change the world. The next question was: Is disability awareness/diversity training the best way to do it? After all, I'm an activist, I have a law degree, I do demonstrations and get arrested when something makes me unhappy enough. This was so, well, nice.

I think that here is where I'm supposed to present a political and academic analysis of why I chose diversity training as the most effective way of attaining social change for people with disabilities at the dawn of the millennium. It would be factually accurate and, of course, impeccably reasoned. It would also not be the truth. At least it wouldn't be the entire truth. The main reason that I chose awareness training is that I had a gut feeling that if done right, it would be an effective method of reaching people who might not have otherwise been reached. I also saw untapped potential in the concept—at least there was untapped potential in the way that I had presented it.

The thought of creating a forum on a regular basis where I could talk to people about my experience of disability absolutely intrigued me. I would have a laboratory where I could try out ideas and activities that might enable participants to begin to reverse an acculturation process that has taught us all to unconsciously and sometimes consciously devalue people with disabilities. I would be forced to challenge and substantiate my assumptions about why people with disabilities are treated the way they are in our society. The most exciting part, although I was not aware of it at the time, was that I would have the opportunity to explore the experience of disability in numerous settings with people from many segments of American society.

Mostly, it seemed like it would be fun…

Was awareness training the most effective method of achieving social change? Probably not, but that didn't matter. What does matter is that it is an effective method. No single strategy or technique is the best choice in all situations at all times. Besides, I was still training lawyers and potential litigants in disability rights law, as well as working with activist groups. There are probably people who think that I have sold out. I don't think so. For one, I like to think that if I had sold out I would have made more money. Second, how are we ever going to change anything if some of us aren't willing to talk to people?

In the very beginning of this process, a colleague said that the question that I should be asking myself about disability awareness training is "awareness of what?" In other words, what were my goals? What changes did I anticipate facilitating in people who had done a training? Were these expectations realistic? More fundamentally, what did I want to communicate to audiences during the course of a training? Certainly, these are valid questions.

There were two things that I wanted audience members to take away from a training. I wanted them to get the issue and I wanted them to change their behavior. If a portion of those two things happened in a training, I would consider it successful.

By "getting it" about disability I mean having a rudimentary understanding about what it is like to have a disability in our society. This could be accomplished by providing participants with information. The information that I wanted people to have was basic. I wanted them to know that people with disabilities are an oppressed group and that this is manifested in numerous ways. The behavioral change that I sought was a little more complex. I wanted participants to come to treat people with disabilities as equals. This behavior could only come about when participants became comfortable with people who have disabilities.

People with Disabilities Are Oppressed

Oppressed is a loaded term and I use it deliberately. People sometimes get defensive when they hear the word. It implies to them that they are part of an intentional conspiracy to disenfranchise and otherwise hurt people. I can understand this reaction because I believe that *oppressing* is not something that the vast majority of people do. But if by oppression you mean unnecessary institutionalization; isolation from the political process; denial of equal opportunity in education, employment, housing, transportation and exclusion from most places that people go ranging from the grocery store to the art museum; then it is an indisputable fact that people with disabilities are oppressed. Not wanting to sound particularly Marxist, I use the word *oppression* judiciously in trainings.

I wanted participants to understand that the negative experiences of people with disabilities are not simply the result of so-called *attitudinal barriers* that can be eradicated in a three-hour training. The phrase attitudinal barriers implies a problem that can quickly and easily be fixed, like ramping a step, rather than a complex phenomenon that needs to be unlearned over a long period of time. Discrimination against people with disabilities is the result of *ableism*, a power dynamic that is parallel to racism, sexism, or homophobia. I define ableism as oppression on the basis of physical, mental, or emotional ability. If participants do not grasp this concept, they are more likely to see the ADA not as civil rights law, but as legislation that requires that people are nice to "the handicapped." Participants need to understand the concept of ableism or at least appreciate the reality of disability discrimination in order to comprehend the consequences of what I call everyday discrimination and more egregious forms of exclusion.

Ableism also ranges from unconscious expressions of condescension to forced sterilization and institutionalization, just as expressions of racism can range from naming a peach color crayon *flesh* to segregation and slavery. Ableism is apparent in the built environment. Until very recently, architectural access wasn't even considered in designing and constructing buildings. It still is often done poorly or not at all. Ableism is apparent in the images that we see in the media as well as in the absence of those images of people with disabilities in the media.

One of the challenging things about communicating the concept of ableism is that unlike racism or the other *isms*, ableism is typically not enacted as a conscious expression of hatred. It is easy to see that a *whites only* sign is a deliberate irrational exclusion of a group of people based on prejudice. It is more difficult to make that argument about a flight of stairs. My challenge was to get participants to draw parallels between the effect of the exclusion created by a *whites only* sign and the effect of the exclusion created by a flight of stairs. This emphatically doesn't mean that the results of each are the same, merely that there are points of comparison. Too often people have decided that because ableism is not always conscious it is not destructive.

A major concern that I had was that the more egregious forms of oppression or discrimination would get lost in short trainings to an audience not particularly conversant in the issues. I could easily imagine having them understand that it was a bad idea not to hire someone just because they used a wheel chair. I am hopeful that most people know this already. Understanding that someone with severe mental retardation should not live in an institution was harder. Even a two-day training cannot begin to scratch the surface of the ways in which society is broken regarding its treatment of people with disabilities. This is one of the limits of training, but I'll talk more about that later…

The fact that people with disabilities are oppressed can be presented in lots of ways. Unless the audience has an expressly political agenda, such as multi-culturalism, feminism (another word that unfortunately has become loaded) or some other social justice issue, I tended not to include specific modules on oppression or what I usually referred to as discrimination. However, the concept, as you'll see in the section on training activities, was always integral to any presentation. Typically, I wove the concept into the training through anecdotes and activities.

I wanted ableism or discrimination or just plain unfairness or whatever else they wanted to call it to be a tangible experience to participants. I wanted them to be specifically aware of concrete and subtle ways that people with disabilities are excluded from participation in our society. I wanted them to understand that laws exist to protect people from some of this treatment, but that they had not yet fulfilled their promise. I wanted them to know that as a result of this exclusion, people with disabilities had been injured. The way that they thought of themselves, their sense of self-esteem and their expectations of themselves had often been altered. I wanted them to know that it hurt not being able to go to the library or school or the museum, whether or not you were consciously barred from participation. I wanted them to know that individuals with disabilities had formed a social movement that has brought about some of the most sweeping civil rights legislation in two decades. I wanted to make people with disabilities visible.

In Order To Reduce Oppression/Discrimination, People Must Make Behavioral Changes

It was important to me that people come away from trainings not only with new insight into the experience of people with disabilities, but with a clue as to how they could change their behavior. I believe that most non-disabled people are terrified of people with disabilities. They are terrified that they will say or do the Wrong Thing. (By the way, many people with disabilities are equally afraid of people who have disabilities that are different from their own.) My theory was that if I could get people to relax even a little about disability they would stop getting in their own way. It wasn't going to be possible to change behavior without reducing discomfort. (Have you ever noticed how discomfort has become a code word for *fear?*)

The other challenge (I won't even go into what that is a code word for) was going to be getting people to want to change their behavior. After all, no one wants to change, otherwise they would have already done it. As I developed training activities, I kept in mind the need to be able to articulate clear and understandable benefits for participants.

Okay, perhaps I wouldn't be able to communicate all of this in a one to eight hour training. But it was important for me to clarify the issues for myself.

TRAINING ACTIVITY: WORD ASSOCIATION

Now that I had actual goals in mind and what I hoped would be a core training activity—the masks—I could begin to think about other training modules. First, I needed to develop an opening activity, one that got people talking and wasn't threatening but, of course, had substance. The activity I chose I call Word Association. Notice that I say chose, rather than created, because I'm pretty sure that I stole it from my friend and colleague Julie Reiskin. I think, but I'm not positive, that she lifted it from someone else.

In Word Association, I write a word on newsprint and ask the audience to share any words, thoughts, feelings, ideas or images that come to mind. The first words that I put up are *disability/handicap.* I make sure that I tell them that calling out an association doesn't necessarily mean that they believe or are in any way endorsing the association. Without too much coaxing most audiences will offer associations. The associations vary from *ramps* and *Stevie Wonder* to *limited* and *uncomfortable.* Then I do the same process with words like mental illness/psychiatric disability, deaf, blind, mental retardation and learning disability. Not surprisingly, mental illness usually elicited the most negative responses such as fear, danger, violent, etc. One surprise was that the word *blindness* almost universally got the response *fear*. This wasn't fear as in being scared of blind people; this was fear in terms of "I don't want this to happen to me." A blind colleague told me about a study that found that after getting cancer, the possibility of becoming blind was the thing that Americans feared most.

This activity quickly gets myths, stereotypes and misconceptions out in the open with relatively little pain. I keep the newsprint of associations on the wall. At the end of the training, I review them to see if the participants' perceptions have significantly changed. They usually have.

Training Activity: Masks

Masks form the basis of the activity on which I have built the rest of the training. I usually present three of the following four masks when I train. The mask presentation is mostly improvisational, though characters say similar things from training to training. The time that each one takes depends on the length of the training and what they have to say on a given day.

The Saint

The first mask that I usually wear is the Saint. She has a smooth blue-white face with flicks of glitter. As I put on the mask, I say, "Sometimes we see people with disabilities as saints…"

I am holy. One of God's children.

I am not gifted with great beauty or intellect or talent.

But I do have some special gifts.

I am very patient.

I can wait for anything.

Forever.

I never get angry for any reason. That would be pointless.

There isn't much I can do that is valuable in the real world.

There are some things, though.

I can do volunteer work in my community. I am very good at helping.

Sometimes I can even work for pay at some little job as long as I am protected from any danger or responsibility.

See, if I saw the real dog-eat-dog world out there, I don't know, I'd crumble.

So, be nice to me. Exchange pleasantries, but whatever you do, don't let me get too close. I might see too much. If I knew what you were really like—how you got angry or jealous or petty sometimes—I'd just be devastated.

So, keep a friendly distance. Remember that your most important job is to protect me from you and the world at all costs.

The Monster

The monster mask is red and green. Its surface is rough and has numerous bumps and protrusions. As I put on the mask, I say, "Sometimes we see people with disabilities as monsters…"

LOOK AT ME. LOOK AT MY FACE.

Imagine having this face twenty-four hours a day, three hundred and sixty-five days a year for what seems like an eternity. How bitter would you be?

How would you feel about the pretty people worried about their suntans and their hairstyles and losing those pesky ten pounds?

I repulse you, don't I? I'm so different from you.

It's as if I'm from another species. I'm like one of those hideous bugs that lives deep in the jungle, almost an alien life form.

But look a little closer…

Maybe we're not as different as you'd like to think. Haven't you ever been just a little afraid of how ugly you look in the mirror in the morning? Especially lately?

Do you ever wonder what changes time will bring? You don't have to be born like this you know; you could have an accident or maybe nature just won't treat you that well as time passes.

I don't see anyone out there getting any younger…

But for now, ignore me. You pretend to tolerate me. But we both know that it's a lie. Leave me alone. Scorn me if you must. But spare me your pity.

Don't even try to include me in your world. We both know that it is one of which I can never be a part.

The Hero

The hero mask is bright yellow with a purple band across the eyes and nose. As I put on the mask, I say, "Sometimes we see people with disabilities as heroes…"

I'm able to leap tall staircases with a single bound!

You know, there are people out there who call themselves *handicapped* or *disabled*.

One thing that I want to get straight right away is that I'm not one of them.

I am merely slightly physically inconvenienced.

See, I've overcome my handicap.

I just pulled myself up by my bootstraps. I don't let anything stop me!

If I use a wheelchair I can push myself across the country.

Walked across the state with one leg.

I don't need an interpreter when I'm deaf; I just read everyone's lips. I don't need Brailled material—I just figure things out. See, I'm a little smarter than most…

I am so sick of these so-called disabled people whining and complaining all the time. Ramps this. Interpreters that. Why can't they just be more like me?

So, don't change anything for me. If a building is inaccessible, don't build a ramp for me. I'll find a way in. Don't bother with an interpreter. You don't even have to include me if you don't want; it's not important.

It is important that you don't give me special treatment.

That would only injure my pride and pride is the most important thing.

So remember, I don't need anything from you.

Except maybe your approval…

The Crusader

The Crusader's face is solid smooth lavender. The letters ADA and the numbers 504—another disability rights law—appear in red letters on her forehead as if carved into her face. I tend to only present her to audiences with disabilities because this particular mask resonates most strongly with them. As I put on the mask, I say, "Sometimes we see people with disabilities as crusaders…"

Do you believe that guy???

Overcome his handicap, yeah, right. As if crawling into a building or missing half of the conversation makes his disability go away!

He betrays all of us every time he opens his mouth.

I am proud to be a person with a disability. I make it my life's work to fight for the rights of all my brothers and sisters with disabilities.

See, it is my duty to represent them. I'm one of the lucky ones. I have a little more privilege than most of them. I've got a good education. I'm relatively bright.

So, I devote my life to fighting for my people.

I will let you do almost anything to me in the name of protecting our rights or improving our condition.

It's okay to carry me up the stairs as long as I get to tell you why it is demeaning and illegal for you to do that.

So, use whatever language you want around me. Don't worry about offending me. I'm not shy and I'm pretty tough. It is more important that you respect my people than you respect me…

After I present the masks, I challenge participants to tell me what the characters have in common. Each monologue has a series of rationalizations for why non-disabled people don't have to include people with disabilities. It would hurt their pride or overwhelm them or be too painful. All represent false images that we place on people with disabilities. Sometimes, people with disabilities take on these masks themselves. I ask participants why they think that people with disabilities might willingly take on a mask. One explanation that I offer is that a known, perhaps more positive, chosen stereotypical role might be preferable to one that is randomly assigned. For instance, I'd rather be seen as the Hero or the Crusader than as, say, the Monster.

I share with audiences the fact that I have worn each of these masks at various points in my life as well as a few others that I did not include here. The Crusader mask was hard for me to take off after her presentation. In fact it wasn't until very recently that I took off the Crusader mask at all.

2

Trainers Just Want to Have Fun

After presenting a lot of awareness training, something changed. I began to get comfortable in front of an audience. This surprised me because, prior to this, I hadn't realized that I had been anything other than comfortable in front of a group. It wasn't so much that I was actively uncomfortable, although I sometimes got nervous when I first started doing legal trainings. But I wasn't actively comfortable either. I knew that I was actively comfortable one time when, on the second day of a two-day legal training, someone said something that struck me as funny and I started laughing uncontrollably. It wasn't nervous laughter, but deep laughter that happens when something is amusing and I'm a little bit punchy. It was as if we were in my living room with friends, not the hotel ballroom du jour.

When I became comfortable, my trainings evolved. I became less concerned with myself and more concerned with the audience. I didn't worry as much about how I looked or sounded. I was less preoccupied with the group's approval. I was more focused on whether or not they were getting the message. Being genuinely comfortable gave me freedom.

I was freer to be spontaneous. I could change plans in the middle of a training should the need arise. I could cut short an activity if it wasn't working or expand one if it really was. If I sensed that an activity or category of activities wasn't going to work, I could ditch them and do another back-up exercise. It was because I had gotten comfortable doing training that I could make up an activity on the night before a major corporate training without testing it or even asking anyone their opinion about it and not worry. The ability to be spontaneous gave me the ability to listen to a group, make an honest assessment and tailor my presentation to best meet their needs.

It's like this. If I was married to the idea of presenting a certain set of activities during a training, I couldn't look at an audience and see that what I was doing or was about to do probably wasn't going to work. I'd almost have to engage in a certain degree of denial and hope for the best. Once I was comfortable—that is, no longer afraid of an audience—I could look them in the eye, make an assessment and not have to wait for their post-training evaluations to see where I had failed to reach them. I was less afraid to think on my feet. If the energy in a room gravitated toward a certain area, I could go with it rather than fight against it in the interest of sticking to the script. With the exception of some of the legal ones, my trainings were never heavily scripted.

The more I relaxed, the more fun I had. This empowered participants to have fun...

This chapter is called "Trainers Just Want to Have Fun" because I think that for the trainer—and, okay, the audience—having fun is the most important part of a training. Why? Well, for one thing, if I'm going to invest huge amounts of time doing something, I want to have a good time. I already earned my boredom chits in law school. If having fun wasn't a priority I'd be a litigator. In order for me to have a good time, I need the people around me to be relatively engaged. That's where the audience having fun comes in.

There are some less selfish reasons that I want trainings to be fun. People learn more easily when they are having a good time. This is something that educators have known and mostly ignored for years. In disability diversity training, we are asking participants to do something that no one wants to do, that is, change. Change is inherently threatening to most people. The lighter I can make the environment, the less threatening it is and the easier it is to absorb and integrate material.

In our society, fun has become a much-maligned concept. It is as if having fun trivializes the issue at hand. I've met people who don't think that training or other activities that have the goal of promoting social justice should be fun. They argue that protection of civil rights is serious and important. This is true. There is nothing funny about ableism or any form of human oppression. Where I disagree is the premise that we must be grim and "appropriate," whatever that means, while learning ways that discrimination manifests itself and somber as we explore ways to change behavior. I have a friend who refers to such anti-fun individuals as having an irony deficiency.

At the risk of sounding like a Pollyanna, a training is an occasion to celebrate because, for whatever reason, there is a roomful of people who are at least tangentially willing to look at their own attitudes and those of others or to learn about the law for the time that you've been allocated. Yes, sometimes they are there because their boss or someone else in power made them attend. Sometimes they are resentful because they have a preconceived notion of what will happen during the event and feel it isn't a good use of their time. They might feel guilty because they don't know all of the answers already and feel that they should. I, as the trainer, have been given an opportunity, a gift as it were. So why not have fun?

Humor and a sense of fun can breathe life into an audience. Until an audience comes to life, very little real change or learning happens. The primary thing that I do to encourage participants to have fun is to have a good time myself. I find that groups will take on and mirror my own attitude.

One technique that I use to facilitate this spirit of fun I stole from my friend Beth, who is an excellent rape crisis trainer. Yes, she has the goal of making rape crisis management trainings fun. I give out what I call Fabulous Prizes. They are silly, cheap little toys that serve no other purpose than to make participants laugh or at least smile. I often use toys that are given out at children's birthday parties.

At the beginning of each training, I go over two Ground Rules which set the tone of the event. The first is to ask questions; I remind participants that if they have a question at least two other people in the room have the same question, but aren't brave enough to ask it. The next rule is to have fun. At this point I share with them my belief that fun expedites the learning process. I tell them that in order to facilitate fun, I will be awarding Fabulous Prizes to participants who ask and answer questions. They don't have to answer questions correctly; they just have to be brave enough to respond. I tell them that one lucky participant may leave with a Brand New Car. It's smaller than a matchbox, but it will definitely fit in those tiny garage spaces reserved for compact cars.

I've learned a lot about participants through the use of Fabulous Prizes. For instance, Fabulous Prizes confirmed my suspicion that not only do trainers want to have fun, so do audiences. In fact, they crave it. One of the commonalties that I've noticed across class, race, culture, age and political lines is that people (with very few exceptions) like getting toys.

How they relate to the toys gives me information. If someone is playing with a plastic dinosaur on their training table, I know that they are pretty comfortable in the room. The more comfortable they are, the more open to learning. Some people get embarrassed and quickly put their toys away. Some people ask me for extra toys so that they can give them to each of their children. I gladly do this, but I'd rather that they keep the toys and play with them themselves. Other frugally minded people try to give back the prizes at the end of the training, ostensibly to save me from buying more. These people I worry about a little. Not so much about their training experience, but the sense of fun in their lives in general.

Toys are disarming. One of the positions taken by the right wing is that we civil rights activists, especially feminists, take ourselves way too seriously and are angry about stupid things; moreover all our alleged problems would go away if we would just lighten up already. It is harder to dismiss a trainer as just a hostile bleeding heart liberal who wants to impose her agenda of political correctness on the world when you've just handed out a plastic harmonica. Despite the levity, the core issues remain. People with disabilities are members of a group that has historically been discriminated against and we, a society, are fundamentally uncomfortable with people who have disabilities.

The obvious risk is that participants might decide that I am frivolous and making light of the experience of human oppression. I haven't found that to be the case. Audiences tend to realize that trainers and participants can take issues seriously without necessarily taking themselves too seriously.

One of the questions that I explored during the pilot training and continue to explore through various incarnations of disability diversity training is: *What do people need in order to change their behavior?* The most obvious answer is information. They need information that the problem, whether it be called discrimination or ableism, exists in many forms, some of which are conscious, some of which aren't. They need to know that, intentionally or not, they participate in this problem. Most important, they need to know that there is behavior they can change that can reduce discrimination.

This being the case, the next issue becomes deciding what is the most effective means of conveying information. I've spent the last seven years experimenting with various ways to do this. The question comes down to: *What do people need in order to be able to learn?* Much has been written about different types of learners. Some people learn orally, others visually, some tactually and others a combination thereof. This is important and I wish that more schoolteachers paid more attention to this research. I can't say that in developing the training I sat down and deliberately created or stole so called multi-modality activities, though I probably promised to do this in my grant. Being an oral learner, I secretly believe that this is the only way that people really learn. Through no fault of my own, I happened to develop or borrow activities that would engage a variety of learners.

The mechanics of how a training is presented is certainly important. But, if I had to pick a single criterion that enabled an audience to learn, it would be having an open heart. People don't learn as easily when they are frightened, angry, guilty or defensive in any other way. It makes sense. You can't absorb information as easily when a large percentage of your energy is being devoted to protecting yourself. So, one of the primary challenges of any diversity training is to present difficult and usually painful information without invoking defensives on the part of participants while at the same time not whitewashing the material.

The bottom line is that I believe that training is a healing process. It begins to heal the wounds of those who have been mistreated. It also begins to heal the injuries of those who have been doing the oppressing or at least contributed to the dynamic by virtue of the fact that they live in an injurious society. I can see colleagues and other individuals who are committed to social justice wincing at the idea that the oppressors are also the oppressed, but bear with me. Yes, of course it is harder to be powerless and oppressed than it is to be someone who is participating in or just witnessing discrimination. I really don't want to get into a discussion about why it is worse to be a member of one group than another. Besides, we'll talk about that when we get to people with disabilities and other minority groups. So, hold on.

One of the useful things that can happen in a training is that participants can give up some of their guilt about how they have treated people with disabilities. Giving up guilt is a healing process. Once people give up guilt, they usually give up resentment. This, too, is healing. Maybe then, and probably not until then, can they change behavior and even call other people and institutions to task when necessary.

I don't mean to suggest that trainings should be touchy-feely sessions where people acknowledge social injustice, are told that they are not responsible for it and go home less guilty but unchanged. Participants need to begin to take responsibility for their attitudes, actions and inactions. But the reality is that the glitziest, most well-researched training techniques and modalities don't work unless people are open.

So what can be done to bring an audience to open their hearts? The more alive an audience is, the easier it is for them to open their hearts. By alive I mean present, engaged and excited. This is one of the relatively few occasions in my life where I've developed a set of rules or at least guidelines.

Ways of Bringing an Audience to Life

1. Be alive yourself.

2. Have fun.

3. Be passionate about your subject. For the duration of the training, it must be the most important thing to you.

4. Be open.

5. Listen.

6. Be willing to change your behavior, both in terms of every day self-transformation and midstream training approach.

7. Absolutely believe that participants should be at the training and that it is the most valuable use of their time.

8. Believe that participants can and will change negative behaviors and beliefs.

9. Find joy in bringing this material to participants.

10. Believe in the magic of training.

These things are easier said than done. Sometimes presenting a training is like enjoying a science fiction movie. You have got to suspend disbelief. So, even though your mind tells you that the woman who comes into your training won't learn—she has announced that the only reason she is there is because her boss or teacher or some other authority figure made her—you must believe that she will. Pretending that you believe this is not enough. You have to actually believe it, at least for the duration of the training.

Liking participants helps. For the most part, I like most people who I encounter. But, frankly, some people are hard to like. The person who is overtly hostile in a training or the one who doesn't need to be there because she understands it all better than me and could present all of this material much more effectively are examples. Sometimes I just ignore these people. I said that liking people helps, not that it is mandatory. Other times, I try to find something that I have in common with them. Maybe we talk about our kids during the break or how hideous the traffic is or our mutual abysmal senses of direction. This can help.

Do you have to be up all the time in order to be a good trainer? Hell, no. Keep in mind that I'm only presenting my way of doing things and as much as I hate to admit it, there are other ways. As my family and friends would tell you, I can be the original depressive cynic. I'm just not that way during trainings. Am I insincere? Almost never—possibly when you give me a gift that I don't like. The truth is that I am energized by the act of presenting. It really is my idea of a good time. So, even though I might be jaded or depressed or exhausted going into a training, I rarely, if ever, come across that way. In case you haven't figured it out, I'm a performer at heart.

TRAINING ACTIVITY: ETIQUETTE AND LANGUAGE

My very first awareness training when I was in high school in the late 70s was solely about etiquette, as in: What do you do when you run into a person with a disability on the street? Should you hold open a door? When should you assist someone with a disability? And what the hell should you refer to them as anyway? Throughout the years and regardless of the kind of organizations where I am training it is remarkable that participants still have the exact same questions.

So, where I might be more intrigued by discussing archetypes and disability or the difference between sympathy and compassion, participants still want and need to know whether or not it is okay to use the word see in front of a blind person. So, I oblige them. It is by no means the entire training, but almost always a portion of it.

Rather than presenting a list of "dos and don'ts" during a training I try to develop scenarios that teach skills as well as etiquette. For example, I present participants with a situation where they take on the role of the receptionist in an organization. A person approaches them and clearly has a question. But the person has a severe speech disability and the listener can't understand a word that the person is saying. I ask participants what they would do.

The first thing I tell participants to do in a situation like this is to relax. I have personally noticed a correlation between my anxiety level and my ability to decipher challenging speech. I suspect that this is true for other people, as well. After they have taken a deep breath or two I suggest that they try to make out a word. After this, they can ask the person with the disability if they got it right. I tell participants that there are many ways to communicate with a person who has a speech disability. Communication aids include a communication board—a board with letters of the alphabet and commonly used words and phrases on it—or a computer or one may ask a coworker for interpretation.

The main guideline is to be respectful of the disabled person. This means looking at and talking to the person with the disability, even if he or she is being interpreted by someone else. They should treat the person as an intelligent adult and not be patronizing. People have a tendency to assume that people with speech disabilities also have mental retardation, which is usually not the case. I tell audiences about the time I went out with a group of colleagues and the assistant director of a non-profit organization who had a speech disability was not given a menu because it was assumed that she could not read. The dynamic is pretty interesting when you think about it. It goes like this. I'm nervous and I can't understand a word that you say, so you must not be very intelligent.

Sometimes I develop additional *hypotheticals* and tailor them to the training setting. By hypotheticals, I mean made-up situations that will help me illustrate a point. But most of the teaching comes from questions that participants ask or their responses to my questions. I might ask participants if they were ever in a situation where they were unsure of what to do or how to act in front of a person with a disability. Just about everyone can remember a situation where this has come up. Generally, people are dying to ask about the time they think that they did the Wrong Thing. Lots of people still carry shame around about what they perceive to have been an insensitive or inappropriate comment that they may have made to someone with a disability many years ago. The irony is that much of the time the comment wasn't inappropriate or was rather inconsequential in the great scheme of things in the life of a person with a disability. What is of significance is how that instance can haunt the non-disabled person and interfere with later interactions.

I frequently find myself in a role that I certainly didn't anticipate. I have become the absolutionist. It turns out that my Catholic upbringing has come in handy. I tell participants that what they did was okay or, if it wasn't, I tell them that they made an honest mistake and can now choose to change their behavior. But I let them know that beating themselves up about it is unnecessary and counter-productive. It is amazing to me how people crave forgiveness. I don't even make them do penance.

I do not mean to suggest that insensitive remarks are never hurtful to people with disabilities. Depending on the nature of the remark or the person's frame of mind about life and their disability on that particular day, the wrong comment can be devastating. My point is that lots of times people without disabilities worry about comments that were relatively innocuous.

The question that frequently arises is "When should I assist people with disabilities?" I tell participants that it is okay to offer help if someone with a disability looks like he or she might need assistance. I ask them to do a reality check as to whether or not someone seems in need of assistance or the person without the disability is projecting this need out of their own anxiety. For example, they see someone who is blind crossing a busy city street. Does the person really look like she or he is in trouble? Or, is the sighted person thinking, "I could never do that if I were blind, that person must need help," ignoring the fact that the person looks confident and has been doing this successfully for most of his or her life?

The other point that I stress is that permission from the disabled person should always be granted before help is given except in the case of a dire emergency, for example in the situation of a blind person about to step out in front of a bus. Should the person with a disability decline help, his or her wish should be respected. Sometimes, participants get hung up because they are uncomfortable offering assistance. The guideline that I give them is that if they offer assistance that they believe someone with a disability actually needs, it is the problem of the disabled person if he or she gets upset or angry.

One audience member told me that she would never offer assistance to a person with a disability because a few years prior to the training, she stopped a blind person from doing something dangerous at the subway station and got yelled at. She had been feeling angry and guilty since that event. I thanked her for telling her story and told her that this kind of sharing is what made for effective training. Then I asked her if a person with blonde hair had ever been rude to her on the subway. She said, "Probably." I asked her if a woman had ever been rude to her on the subway. "Sure", she replied. I then asked her if she was still mad at people with blonde hair and women. She and the rest of the group got my point. We went on to have a great discussion about assumptions and beliefs based on single interactions. It might seem evident that you shouldn't generalize one person's behavior to an entire group of people, but somehow this sophisticated corporate audience hadn't internalized this premise.

Occasionally, if asked, I will hand out an etiquette cheat sheet with tips for hanging out with people with disabilities. This isn't a substitute for actual training, but it gives people a point from which to start. The cheat sheet usually has some dos and don'ts and includes advice on language.

Language is a funny thing, because at the risk of being labeled a slave to political correctness, I think that the words that we use to describe people and situations are very important. I think that it is of the utmost importance to call people by the name that they wish to be called. On the other hand, I hate to see people, particularly training participants, tongue tied by the fear of using incorrect language to the point where they become unable or unwilling to communicate. So, the rule that I establish is that for the duration of the training it is okay for participants to call me and anyone else with a disability anything that they want. If they are interested, I will tell them about my preferences about language and what the general, but not complete, consensus is in the disability rights movement. I discuss the power of language and why I think it is important to call people what they want to be called.

There are other peculiarities of language. Sometimes, the same words mean radically different things to different groups of people. Take, for instance, the word "special." For the longest time, I had difficulty getting audiences to understand why I and other people with disabilities bristle at the word. Why couldn't they see that the word was at best patronizing and at worst demeaning?

They couldn't see it because this was not their experience of the word. For the fun of it one day, I wrote the word special on some newsprint and asked participants to call out what associations they had

with the word. To them, special was a good thing. It had positive connotations. They associated it with being unique or noteworthy.

I asked them if they wanted to know my associations with the word.
Having no choice, they said, "Yes." I told them that I associated "special" with situations where people with disabilities were segregated and
offered substandard or less than equal circumstances, as in special education or special passengers lounge in an airport. It was also a euphe-
mism used to describe people who are not as good as the norm as in
people with special needs. Special needs children are the less desirable,
harder to adopt kids. Special Olympians are athletes with disabilities
who couldn't compete in the regular competitive Olympics. The truth
is that people with disabilities don't have special needs. They have the
same needs as everyone else. It is just that they might need an accessible
environment or services in order to have their not so special basic
human needs met.

Regardless of where participants stood on issues such as segregated
versus integrated services, the incontrovertible fact was that at least
some people, including myself, had bad associations with the word
"special" when used to describe them. Suddenly, these people who did
not understand what my problem was with the word "special" had
fresh insight into my perspective. Guess what happened? They got it.

Another example of a phrase that is neutral to most non-disabled
people but loaded for people with disabilities, at least those of us who
are old enough to call ourselves baby boomers, is the phrase "fire hazard." Sometimes in strategizing access solutions someone will come up
with a potential solution that violates fire code. This is just about
always inadvertent. But I've been in rooms where people with mobility
and other disabilities cringe at the use of the phrase "fire hazard." Is
this because we're terminally cranky and have some convoluted reason-
ing for why this is politically incorrect terminology? Perhaps, but more
likely it is because this has been used as a justification for exclusion
since our childhood. That's why they told us we couldn't go to school,
eat in a restaurant, or go to the movies. We were fire hazards. Since

then we've learned to make jokes about people with disabilities that spontaneously combust, but the memory did its damage.

Obviously, not all people with disabilities speak English as their native language and there are a host of other cultural idioms that might communicate different things to different people. When someone with a disability speaks Spanish or Japanese as their native language, this at minimum is acknowledged, if not well tolerated. But there is a group of people with disabilities who do not speak English as their native language and this fact is by and large unknown. They are deaf people whose native language is American Sign Language, or ASL, as it is known. Most people think of sign language as a set of gestures and hand shapes that are a code for English. While this is true for some types of sign language, such as signed English, it isn't the case with ASL. ASL has grammar, word order, and syntax that is independent of English. There are even grammatical devices found in ASL that do not occur in English.

Aside from the fact that this is interesting, why do I make sure that I bring this up in training? It is simple. Without this information, it is easy to miscommunicate with deaf people whose native language is ASL. From this miscommunication, participants might come to the conclusion that deaf people, or at least the deaf person that they are dealing with, are not very bright.

This is the story that I use to illuminate the idea that ASL is a language in and of itself. When I was in college, I took a course in sign language linguistics. The class was about equally divided between hearing and deaf students. One day the teacher came in and signed a joke as she spoke. It was moderately amusing and all of the hearing students laughed. All of the deaf students, who happened to be native ASL signers, looked at her blankly. The hearing students were secretly harboring seriously politically incorrect thoughts about the intelligence and or sense of humor among deaf people. Then, the professor told another joke and this time the deaf students laughed uproariously and the hearing students sat silently wondering what her point was. Her point was that she had told two jokes, both of which used idiom that didn't translate into the other language.

Participants need this information when they are determining whether or not to provide a sign language interpreter or are confused by a note written by a native signer.

3

Venturing Out—Taking the Show on the Road

Beginning the process of presenting awareness trainings was challenging. There was only so much preparation that I could do. Eventually, I had to go out on my own and present training by myself without a net. Actually, there was a net of sorts. Through my grant from the Boston Globe Foundation I had the opportunity to pilot-test my trainings. *Pilot* is a great word that is used to describe trainings with material that is new and still being evaluated. The concept is freeing in that should people find it abysmal, you have the license to somewhat righteously say, "It was only a pilot training."

As soon as I'd put together a few activities, I had nothing left to do but try 'em out. Creating activities to be theoretically presented was much different than doing it in reality. For one thing, theoretical training is much less scary. My very first pilot training was, well, memorable. I had no idea how much material I had relative to the time available. It turned out that I had probably six hours of material for a two-hour training. The audience was made up of diversity trainers—nothing is scarier than people who Know What They Are Doing. The setting was a tad intimidating—a meeting room at Boston's Symphony Hall. Oh, and my funder was going to be there.

Did I mention that I was a bit nervous? We—I'm not positive that I was actually involved in this decision—decided to evaluate each module as it was presented. I would present a training segment and at the end participants would, as a group, offer verbal feedback. This gave me the opportunity to hear the initial responses of various audience members. This was interesting in that sometimes they agreed that an activity worked or didn't work; other times, their opinions were diametrically opposed. It also gave me practice in utilizing criticism and not taking it personally. I couldn't get too upset about a comment if I had to turn around and immediately present another activity. Once I got going, the process wasn't nearly as traumatic as I had anticipated. Of course, it helped that the group was merciful.

Afterwards, we disseminated detailed written evaluations. Interpreting evaluations turned out to be more of an art than I had initially realized. What did it mean that a couple of people hated the masks? Should I drop Them and Us (Chapter Five Training Activity) because a highly respected audience member thought that dolls were childish? Should I scrap any of the activities that I had presented for potentially more promising ones that I didn't show because I ran out of time?

The feedback from diversity trainers was a little atypical. Many were more inclined to comment on style and technique than on what they may have learned during the training. One person noticed that my slides were off center on the screen.

Stylistically, I had two problems of which I was aware that they picked up on. First, I speak way too fast. I sometimes joke with audiences that I should have auditioned for the Federal Express commercial popular a few years back where the guy talked really, really fast. Theoretically, this was under my control and fixable. I think that I've improved with practice and discipline, but it is still something that I worry about. I remember being somewhere in the south and having it dawn on me while my co-trainer presented that I spoke rapidly for a Northeasterner. Would they get anything that I said? One thing I have learned to do is to make audiences aware that *I* am aware of this tendency and ask them to remind me to slow down if my pace gets too outrageous.

Once, while I was doing an ADA training in Texas, my assistant and I noticed one woman who seemed to be having a problem with what I said. She kept whispering to the person next to her. Before I let my imagination run too wild with fantasies about how she thought that I, the ADA and maybe even people with disabilities were bad, I took the radical step of talking to her individually during one of the breaks to find out what was actually going on. It turns out that she did have a major problem with me and with the training. She couldn't under-stand a damned thing that this Yankee said. She had been using the woman sitting next to her as a translator.

Training Hint: If audience members look or act confused or uncomfort-able, they probably are. Get brave and ask what the problem is. You might be able to help.

By and large my often rapid-fire staccato speech has mostly proved surmountable. One trainer told me of a study that showed that people can absorb speech at a much quicker rate than they think once they get used to it and that modulating speed was nearly impossible without lots of coaching. I never bothered to track down the study and I have no idea whether or not this is true. But, it made me feel better. Who knows?

My other stylistic problem is related to my disability. My coordina-tion isn't great and I generally have a harder time than most people handling objects. At first, I was terrified of handling the number of props that I use during a training. What if I dropped them? What if my awkwardness in handling them was a huge distraction? If you met me on the street you wouldn't know that I have a disability that affects my coordination, but people have been known to shriek when they see me handle a knife on the rare occasion that I cook. As was the case with many of the training activities, as I got more comfortable, groups that I presented trainings to got more comfortable. So, now if I drop a prop I don't get rattled and neither does the group.

I bring these concerns up because everyone who presents has similar issues that they think could get in their way when presenting. I encour-age anyone with a message and a passion to train. Don't try to remove what you may perceive as an impediment. You probably can't. What you can do is work with it and integrate it into your overall style.

Having taken the plunge and presented my first training, I went ahead and scheduled probably a dozen more pilot trainings at non-profits in Boston. This is where I really came to understand how much time my material took to present and what activities work best with different types of groups. I evaluated audience response and for the most part moderated trainings accordingly, although, as I said, I decided to be patient with some activities such as the Masks and Them and Us to see if audiences would appreciate them more as my technique improved.

The non-profit groups were for the most part a delight. They had good hearts and wanted me to be there. They were open to being field-tested, as it were. This doesn't mean that my work was always easy. I remember in the course of a day going from one group where the majority of participants had graduate degrees in fields like social work and psychology to groups of day care providers who may or may not have had a high school education. My message was the same to both groups; however, my terminology and use of jargon was different.

One of the fun things about presenting to these non-profits was that the audiences and the settings varied greatly. They ranged from arts to social services organizations. Settings included spacious, comfortable conference rooms in fancy buildings, cramped conference rooms where we literally sat toe to toe, and a sleeping area in a homeless shelter. The homeless shelter was particularly interesting. When the director told me that I'd be training in the shelter, I had envisioned a meeting room of some sort. Instead, she brought us into a cavernous room with a few chairs and maybe a hundred cots. My assistant looked a little panicked as we surveyed the sea of cots trying to figure out where to put the slide projector. I was in trainer mode and reassured her that we would figure it out.

We propped up the slide projector on one cot and used another as a makeshift presentation table. There are training professionals, as well as books, that will tell you about optimal learning environments for people who they refer to as adult learners. It was at the shelter that I began to realize that the conventional things that I had learned about room size and layout really didn't matter as much as many people would lead you to believe. I tried to keep this in mind when I had an endless debate with a training team and hotel staff about whether an open u or a modified chevron was best for presenting legal training. (For those of you who aren't hotel meeting planners, an open u is a seating arrangement where tables are arranged in a u-shaped formation. A chevron is an arrangement where tables and or chairs are slanted so as to face a center point.) What mattered was that the audience felt at home in the room. Whether it was a cramped meeting room, an art museum, Symphony Hall or a homeless shelter was irrelevant.

Incidentally, one of the most important things I learned during the course of the pilot trainings was the value of an assistant. She would drive; Boston is a two-hour commute for me. She would park the car, which in Boston can take longer than the commute. She would help me carry the ton of stuff that I schlep to trainings. Oh, and if I was using my manual wheelchair, she helped push. This made it possible to do many more trainings in a short period of time than I would have been able to do alone. The first time I had an assistant come with me, it felt uncomfortable and awkward. I felt as if I'd lost some of my independence. The second time she came I couldn't imagine why I had ever wanted to do it alone.

After I had piloted the training without having anyone throw eggs at me, I decided that it was time to take the show on the road and present the training to other audiences, namely anyone who would pay me. At first, I did the training for other non-profits outside of the Boston Globe Foundation's catchment area. Some of the marketing I did on my own and some I did through a disability rights non-profit called Progressive Attitudes. I ended up venturing into two divergent and unlikely audiences at the same time. One audience was the corporate world; the other was an inner city high school.

In retrospect, I had about the same degree of misconception about each type of group. I was warned about each group by earnest colleagues who, by and large, had spent their professional careers working for non-profit organizations or in state government. As I think about it, they gave me pretty much the same warnings. People cautioned me that I didn't speak the same language as "those people"—I came from a different background and my material might not be culturally appropriate. Besides, "those people" are rude and disrespectful and might eat me alive if I wasn't careful. "Those people" would never listen to me because I wasn't one of them. As I said earlier, whenever someone uses the phrase *those people*, you've got problems. I found it amusing that "those people" referred to both inner city teenagers and corporate executives.

The only concern that people expressed to me about high school students that they didn't express about staff in corporations was my ability to dress appropriately. Some feared that I wouldn't be able to dress "street" enough. No one was concerned that I couldn't pass for corporate. In fact some theorized that the appeal of corporate training was getting to buy more clothes. (I'm not quite that shallow.) And no, I never tried to dress street or hip-hop.

Corporate Training

You'll find lots more about training in and working to diversify corporations throughout this book. Because in many ways the corporate environments ended up being so similar to other environments, I've woven anecdotes of my corporate escapades throughout. Who knew?

Training in corporations was sort of the last frontier for me. See, there is this mystique that has developed among non-profit organization types like myself about the Private Sector. For me, there is generally a mystique surrounding any phrase with the word *sector* in it. Corporate types must be smarter, more efficient and generally have their acts more together than those of us in non-profit organizations, government and the rest of the world 'cause they make the big bucks, right?

There was also a way in which they were suspect. Some of the people there may have different values than I did. (Gasp!) They may even have voted differently from me.

Training buddies worried that my material might not be as well received in a corporate environment as in non-profits, state agencies and municipalities. They pointed out that my training was a bit, well, unconventional. Some of them told me this as if they were breaking news to me. I might be a bit of an eccentric, but that doesn't mean that I'm not a self-aware eccentric. Some people thought that I should tone it down just a little for corporate audiences. At first I agreed, but when I looked at what that actually meant I decided against it. Toning the training down would look like abandoning Fabulous Prizes, the masks and possibly becoming less irreverent. This amounted to cutting the heart and soul out of the training. I wasn't willing to do that, at least not until I found out conclusively that a corporate audience couldn't deal with these things.

So, one day I found myself in front of a corporate audience equipped with masks, dolls, and the plastic frogs, miniature harmonicas and yo-yos that I used as Fabulous Prizes. I was prepared. I had been warned. Things here would be Different. I wasn't entirely clear what that meant. I'm not really sure what I had expected. But guess what? Corporate Land wasn't much different from Non-Profit Land, State Agency Land, Municipality Land, University Land or even, as I was about to find out, Inner City High School Land.

The usual characters came to trainings. Some people got it before they had met me, others got it during the training and a few didn't get it at all. Kinda like every other audience…In terms of work habits and practices, some were compulsive workaholics, others were adequate at their jobs, and some didn't seem to quite pull their weight. Again, kinda like every other workplace that I had visited.

As far as the masks, dolls and Fabulous Prizes went, I think that they liked them more than other groups. They liked the masks and dolls better because by the time I got to corporations I was better at conducting the activities. The Fabulous Prizes they just seemed to appreciate more. I do admit to being nervous the first time I handed an executive vice-president a rubber dragon finger puppet, but it was fun.

When I first started doing corporate trainings, I remember an incident where a very serious looking woman sought me out during a training break. I figured that she was going to disclose a hidden disability of her own or ask for advice about a family member with a disability. This wasn't at all unusual. Instead she shyly said, "I hate to bother you, but I was a spokesperson for my activity group and, well, I think that you forgot to give me a Fabulous Prize." I gave her a toy car secure in the knowledge that Fabulous Prizes had not been a mistake at large corporations.

There were some differences between corporate and non-corporate training. With the exception of some of the Ivy League universities that I had worked with, the food served at corporate trainings was better. Hey, this is important when you eat two thirds of your meals on the road. People dressed a little better, except on casual days, which I think they threw in to confuse me.

To my surprise, I had some of my more profound training interactions at corporations. I was particularly struck by a conversation I had with a group about the concept of sympathy. Sympathy is a complex issue. I talk about how people with disabilities don't want sympathy and how pity is almost always destructive despite the good intentions of the individual who is feeling sorry for you. Ordinarily, participants nod faintly in agreement whether they actually understand or not. We are conditioned to believe that sympathy when directed toward ourselves is a bad thing. Often, we feel it is okay to direct it toward others. Most fundraising strategies are dependent on the public's sympathy.

In this particular training, a participant disclosed that his friend had recently been diagnosed with multiple sclerosis and he felt a tremendous amount of sympathy toward her. He wanted to know how and why this was wrong. I explained that no feeling is wrong. Feeling sympathy for an individual who you know well, as in this case, is different from directing it toward an entire group. It is based on real circumstances, not just stereotypical generalizations, as in "Oh, those poor people must be so miserable."

I also told him that from what he had said, I suspected that what he was feeling was a lot closer to compassion than sympathy. People in the group were curious as to the difference. I explained it like this. Sympathy usually involves being nice to the person, having a desire to protect the person, and most important, not regarding the person as an equal because of what is perceived to be his or her unfortunate circumstances. Compassion is acting on empathy that you have toward a person. It may involve being nice, but it also involves acting in the person's best interest. In other words, the sympathetic thing to do with someone who has been newly diagnosed with multiple sclerosis might be to say, "You poor dear, I understand that you can never work again." The compassionate thing to do might be to give them a gentle kick in the butt to get them back to work. The group seemed to understand this.

Then someone brought the discussion up to another level. She remarked that she liked it when people were sympathetic toward her. It made her feel safe and cared for. I asked her to talk more about the circumstances under which she enjoyed sympathy. She said, "You know, when you have the flu and someone fluffs your pillow and brings you chicken soup." I said, "Yes, most people appreciate that from time to time; even people with disabilities appreciate getting taken care of when they have the flu." Then I asked if she would enjoy being treated like that all of the time. Everybody needs an occasional break from responsibility, but most of us don't want to be absolved from it for all time and without our consent. The light bulb went on. We continued to go back and forth about compassion versus sympathy and why sympathy could get in the way of empowering people with disabilities.

Another topic that came up often in corporations was the idea of people with disabilities being inspirational. Many participants did not understand why I saw the concept of elevating people with disabilities as inspirations as a bad thing. I have to admit that it is another tough one to explain. But the explanation goes like this. First, being an inspiration is boring. The implication is that you should spend most of your time being saintly or overachieving depending on the brand of inspirational role that you have been assigned. In either case, there isn't a lot of room for fun.

Second, people with disabilities are usually deemed inspirational for doing normal things. It is acceptable to be inspired when a person with a disability wins the Nobel Prize. But be inspired because they won the Nobel Prize, not because they have a disability or they did it in spite of a disability. Be inspired because he is a brilliant scientist, not because he figured out how to get dressed in the morning without being able to see. I remember a teacher being inspired by how a student got around school in a power wheelchair. This was pretty demeaning because all the kid had to do was push on the joystick on the wheelchair and take off. Praising someone for doing something simple can be devastating to a person's self-esteem. This student inspired me not because of how she used her chair, but by how she survived an educational environment which sought to segregate her in a school without a bathroom that was accessible to her.

The other issue that follows on the heels of people with disabilities being inspirational is that we are brave. By and large, we're no more or less brave than people in general. I liked my husband's response to this. One time, a client got into his car and saw a cane that I sometimes used. He asked what it was for and Ken replied that it was his wife's cane. This guy, who had never met me and up until thirty seconds before had not been aware of my existence, exclaimed, "She's so brave!" Without missing a beat, my husband said, "Actually, she's terrified of spiders."

Bravery suggests a choice. Those of us with disabilities didn't get one. Many, if not most of us, wouldn't have picked the disability option had it been up to us. I think that it was Gerri Jewel, a comedian with cerebral palsy who said, "I don't know why people think I'm brave. It's not like God said, 'You want cerebral palsy?' And I said, 'Great, I'll take it.'"

I think that the underlying dynamic goes something like this. A sighted person sees a blind person crossing a busy intersection in a crowded city. The sighted person thinks, either consciously or unconsciously to him or herself, "I'd be terrified if I had to cross the street without being able to see." The blind person either isn't afraid, which given mobility training is likely, or crosses the street anyway. The sighted person concludes, "She's so brave."

Bravery is a so-called positive stereotype. There are lots more like it. Think about the hero and the saint masks. The stereotypes are rather familiar: people with disabilities are more patient because of what they have gone through; they are God's special children, they have overcome their disability; their other senses are better developed; etc. The problem is that there is no such thing as a truly positive stereotype. Because they are insidious, these stereotypes are in some ways more damaging to people with disabilities then blatantly negative stereotypes. It is easy to see that a stereotype (such as people who use wheelchairs are bitter or that men with mental retardation are sexual predators) is based on prejudice and misconception. It is also easy to understand how these associations hurt people with disabilities. Who wants to be regarded as bitter or as a sex fiend? But because being regarded as courageous or good is on its face a positive thing, it is more difficult to see how this limits people with disabilities. My main point is that any role based on a generalization without taking the individual into account is damaging. What it does is prevent the world from seeing the actual person as she is.

The difference that I appreciated most about training for corporations was that I encountered less guilt and a more straightforward attitude. I think this is because corporations have fewer pretexts of serving the people than do non-profits and government agencies. Sometimes in non-profits there's an attitude of We're-Doing-God's-Work-Already-and-Now-You-Are-Burdening-Us-with-Something-Else.   In fairness, non-profits and government agencies are perpetually under funded so it's understandable why they may give some resistance when told implicitly or explicitly that they must manage to do more with their limited resources. The other challenge is that staffs of these organizations sometimes feel guilty. They believe that because they have a social conscience they should automatically be comfortable with disability and have already fixed any problems that may arise. This doesn't exonerate them from complying with the law or having an understanding of disability issues.

The perspective of corporations is more likely to be: "We have a problem, otherwise we wouldn't be paying you to help us fix it. Now what can we do to change things while increasing the bottom line?" These, of course, are generalizations; not all non-profits and government agencies are guilt-ridden and certainly not all corporations are eager to change, but you get my drift.

TRAINING ACTIVITY: OUT OF THE BOX

I made up Out of the Box over a glass of wine while waiting for my $15 dollar hamburger in the restaurant of the five-star hotel in which the corporation had put me up. This helped compensate for all of the less than five-star hotels I have stayed in when training non-profits. It was Christmastime and I was bored and lonely, so I decided to redesign major portions of the training. I wanted to come up with an interactive activity, in other words, one in which participants do most of the work.

The more that participants are forced to actually think and come to their own conclusions, the more likely it is that the material stays with them. That's my theory, anyway. I'm sure someone has put a lot of time and energy into research proving this. So what could I have them think about?

Since many of the participants are in the position of hiring people or influencing hiring decisions, I decided to develop a job-focused activity. They would become vocational rehabilitation counselors for the day, or at least for a half-hour to forty-five minutes during the activity.

I call this activity Out of the Box because the phrase was popular some time ago in corporate circles or so I'm told. Corporate jargon makes as much sense and changes at least as frequently as teenagers' slang. But my point was that I wanted participants to begin thinking beyond their typical constraints.

In this activity, small groups of people are assigned a person with a disability. As in Who Lives Where? (Chapter Seven Training Activity), they are real people to whom I've given fictitious names. The small groups are asked to act as career counselors for these individuals. They are assigned to think of potential careers that the person could have and brainstorm any resources that might be needed to assist the disabled person in accomplishing his or her goal. Although the adult individuals in question are real people with actual jobs, the purpose of the activity is not to guess what the person does in real life, but to come up with career possibilities.

Some of the people that groups might be assigned include:

Angie, who has multiple personality disorder and a degree from an Ivy League university. Her symptoms include depression, which makes it hard to get out of bed some mornings, and anxiety, which makes traveling even short distances difficult at times. She is interested in human rights, social change and business.

Jeff, who is 16 and has been blind since birth. He is a talented high school student with special aptitude in math and science. His passion is archeology. He has been told that because of his disability, this career would be impossible. He has come to you asking for other ideas given his aptitude, interests, personality and disability.

Jennifer has severe cerebral palsy. It affects all four limbs as well as her ability to speak. She uses a wheelchair, is unable to feed or dress herself, and her speech is difficult for most people to understand. She has a BA in psychology and business.

Tim is nine years old. He has a history of depression and often acts out in school. He can barely read and can do only the simplest arithmetic. He cannot tie his shoes.

First, I have participants break up into small groups. Then I assign them to work with one or two of the individuals profiled above. I give the groups somewhere between fifteen and forty-five minutes, depending on time available and goals of the group, to brainstorm ideas for what these individuals could do for a living. I ask them to think about what support services and/or accommodations the individual or individuals who had been assigned to them would need in order to be successful on the job. I ask them to stretch their assumptions about what people with disabilities can or cannot do and be creative about the types of accommodations or support that these people might need. In other words think "out of the box."

After they work for a while, I have the groups come back together and report what they have come up with. Afterwards, I tell them what the actual people with disabilities ended up doing. Angie is the director of a non-profit organization. She has a personal assistant who helps her with moments that can sometimes be problematic like getting out of bed in the morning, driving to meetings and traveling out of state. Jeff is an adult who I don't know but have read about; he works as an archeologist. Like Angie, Jennifer is also the director of a private, non-profit organization. She uses a personal assistant, speech synthesizer and a communication board in getting her job done.

Tim…most groups have Tim end up as a janitor or working in a fast food restaurant with a job coach. These are certainly honorable jobs, but Tim decided to do something else in life. Tim was a real child. His name was Albert Einstein. Obviously, not every person with a disability will turn out to be a genius. But we should work hard not to underestimate anyone's potential.

TRAINING ACTIVITY: DRAW A CHILD

Draw a Child is a ruse to get participants to look at issues such as race, media images and statistics. If I am going to teach anyone even the most rudimentary statistics, the activity must be fun and craftily camouflage the fact that I am dealing with numbers.

I introduce Draw a Child as the arts and crafts segment of our training. I ask participants to draw a picture of a child with a disability with markers, colored pencils or crayons. The only rule is that this can't be a real child. After they have been working on it for a few minutes, I tell them that I want to know the child's race, gender and disability. When they are done, I ask them to imagine their children as adults. Do they work? If they work, what do they do? What is their general socioeconomic status? Where do they live? Are they married? Do they have a family?

Next, I bring out three of my eighteen-inch preschool aged dolls. I obviously got over the idea that using dolls was inappropriate. One has a white cane and a stuffed guide dog. I know, blind people don't use both at the same time and children that small aren't given guide dogs, but it's damn cute. Another doll has crutches and braces. The third has no apparent disability. One is African American, one is Latino and one is Asian. All are beautiful dolls that were developed using child models. All are smiling.

I introduce the audience to my dolls by name and I describe their disability. I explain that the doll without equipment, Jerry, has a learning disability. I ask participants if the kids that they drew resemble mine or not. Frequently, audience members are struck by the fact that my dolls are smiling and theirs are not. We then have a discussion of images of people with disabilities in the media and how as a culture we've been flooded with images of unhappy people with disabilities.

The next issue that comes up is race. Virtually everyone, regardless of race and regardless of politics, draws a white child. I remember doing one training where a head of Diversity in Human Resources was absolutely befuddled as to why he drew a white child. This African American man wanted to know why he did this. "I never draw white people," he said with a laugh. "What made me do this now?" We talked about the power of images from literature and the media to shape our ideas about disability and the absence of images of people of color in the media.

I then ask them how their kids turned out. This is where statistics are brought up and they get a dose of reality. I ask for a show of hands as to how many of their adult kids were employed when they reached thirty. Almost without fail 100 percent of the kids are working. If they have broken down into groups I have a spokesperson summarize what they do for a living. They are rocket scientists and doctors and teachers and stockbrokers. Virtually everyone makes a middle class or upper middle class living. I congratulate them but tell them that 75 percent of those who raised their hands to indicate that their now adult kids were working would have to put them down. That is the unemployment rate for people with disabilities in this country. And, by the way, because of discrimination, inadequate education and internalized oppression, most of their kids would not be professionals with moderate to high incomes. If they had drawn girls with disabilities, they would have an even higher rate of unemployment and earn less when they did get jobs. If they were people of color, this would again raise their unemployment rate and decrease their wages.

So we enter a discussion of what is referred to as compounded oppression, the dynamic by which the effects of discrimination increase exponentially when factors that incite discrimination are added. Many participants report that their adult kids are married and have children themselves. This is a good opportunity to discuss marriage disincentives and the legal, logistical and social challenges faced by parents with disabilities.

Yes, people with disabilities want to and do get married. Sometimes we get to talk about sex and disability here. However, individuals who get social security are financially penalized for it. Everyone has heard of the octogenarians that are "living in sin" because to do otherwise would chip away at the pittance that they get from social security. Well, the same thing is true for young people with disabilities who collect social security. Even though it is absolutely legal to marry if you have a disability, under certain circumstances, it is discouraged.

Having children is another sticky matter. I usually tell groups that I can and have done entire daylong workshops just about parents with disabilities. For the purposes of this activity, I tell them a few anecdotes to make my point. I tell a story of a competent, fit woman who had a hospital petition to take custody of her baby when she was eight months pregnant. The official grounds were "disability." They were not successful but she went through a few weeks of hell fearing that her baby would be taken away forever. I tell them that I have yet to meet a woman with a known disability who has not on some level had her ability to parent questioned by someone who had a form of authority over such things. Like most things in life, how far they got in removing or threatening to remove the child seems to be directly linked to the woman's age, how much money she had and how white her skin was.

The other story that I tell them is about a bill that was drafted by a state agency in Connecticut that essentially made disability a presumption of parental incompetence. This bill did not pass. In fact, it was withdrawn by the Attorney General right before the public hearing. It helped that around seventy-five parents with disabilities came to testify against the bill.

Although these stories have good outcomes—the pregnant woman kept her child, the bill infringing on parental rights didn't pass—many do not. Lots of parents, particularly women with disabilities, have lost custody of their children because of others' preconceptions and prejudice. But even the instances with positive outcomes have ramifications for people with disabilities. They cause us to be threatened and to see ourselves as other. The knowledge of what could have happened even after you have escaped it can be very frightening. As I wish I had told the legislature—you always think of the really good lines after you testify—I had to miss my son's performance at school that day in order to testify at the hearing. On the way to pick him up after school that day, I had to decide whether or not to tell him where I had been and why I had missed his performance.

People respond more viscerally when these statistics and dynamics affect their personal children even though the children are invented and they have only known them for a few minutes. Shrinkage of their hypothetical children's future causes participants to take notice. I never know what kind of discussions will come out of Draw a Child. That is what makes it so much fun.

4

Adventures in an Inner City High School

A fter I had spent a fair amount of time providing training in non-profit and government organizations, I wrote a grant to provide ADA and disability awareness training to students at a Connecticut high school. With a statewide ADA group, I circulated a Request for Proposal to public high schools throughout the state. The proposition was fairly simple. If they would let us into their school and give us some modicum of support, we would teach their students and faculty about the ADA, architectural access and disability awareness. We would do this for at least one and up to three years. What made this deal even sweeter was that everything offered was free. To my delight, one of the schools that responded was a high school in Hartford. It had a reputation in the media for being a tough school.

It was critical to me that the project take place in a school with a population that had a significant number of people of color. A major problem with the disability rights movement, locally and nationally, is that it is dominated by white people. We bring our white perspective to the table when we draft legislation, make policy and form organizations. The result is that people who are African American, Afro-Caribbean or Latino often feel less than welcome in the movement.

A special education teacher at Hartford's Weaver High School wrote the response to our request. In the application, he reported that the school population was roughly 98 percent African American and 2 percent Latino. Most of the students, though by no means all, were poor. This was exactly the environment in which I wanted to work.

On one hand, Weaver conformed to the stereotype of an inner city high school. Much of the student population lives in projects, students drop out frequently, and (I suspect but have never confirmed) students have a higher rate of teen pregnancy or at least teen births than neighbors in the more lily white suburbs. The physical plant is a large, nearly windowless 1970s building that has deteriorated long before its time. Rumors abound that is was built on swampland that never should have been developed. Teachers and students constantly complain about air quality. A Hartford police officer is stationed at the school during all hours that the school is open.

On the other hand, I never felt anything but safe as a visitor at Weaver. It is one of the few places that I usually did not lock my car. Yes, there were students who acted out and were rude—this was high school after all—but they were the exception. As a whole the student body was unusually respectful. I worked with one student teacher who was making a mid-life career shift to teaching. As fellow outsiders, we compared notes often. He told me that when he first came to Weaver he was shocked at the language. He'd been called words that he had infrequently, if ever, been called elsewhere. He was now regularly called *sir* and *mister*. I remember being similarly shocked on one of the first days I came to the school. Not only did a student hold the door for me, but when I thanked him he said that it was his pleasure. Could it be that manners weren't dead, they were just hiding in city schools?

This was a totally different training arena. What were the kids and, for that matter, the faculty and administration going to make of this thirty-something (read old) white lady who used a wheelchair some of the time? Other old white ladies with disabilities thought that I was pretty strange.

What would they think of the Masks? Could I give them Fabulous Prizes? How would I teach them about the law anyway (that was one of the things that I was funded to do there)? Would any of this have any relevance to them or their lives? These were my midnight and 1 A.M. and 2 A.M. and 4 and 5 A.M. musings in the early days of the project. Fortunately, I was also beginning a national project to teach school administrators about the law and beginning to contemplate corporate training, so I had many other late night conundrums to ponder should I become bored with obsessing about Weaver. Worrying is not what I like to do best, but it is where my innate talent lies.

After a not-as-successful-as-I-would-like-spring, where I tried to recruit students to do the project as an after school activity, a couple of veteran teachers took me under their wings. One taught social studies and another taught tech ed—this used to be shop or industrial arts when I was in school, but students now learn things like design and computer assisted drafting. They gave me incredible access to their classes. I ended up teaching disability awareness, disability rights law and the basics of architectural access in the classroom on an ongoing basis.

My first task was to figure out how to relate to these kids who didn't look, speak or dress like me. While this is true of me and all high school students, there were additional dynamics at work. Face it. I was in a different culture. The good and bad part about this was that I wasn't doing a typical consultant one or two shot deal where I train and run. Some of these kids I would see once a week for an entire semester. Others would be stuck with me for an entire year. To the extent that I had things to say to which they could relate—how on earth would I make this last an entire year?

At first, I was conscious of being one of the only white people in the room. I didn't like the fact that I was aware of this, but I was. It did go away fairly quickly. I noticed this when a teacher was referring to one of a half dozen assistant principals. I was unsure who he was. When I realized whom she was talking about, I thought, "Oh, you mean the white guy."

Presenting to a non-white, non-middle class audience changed the way I trained. It kept me honest. My dolls and slides were of people from multi-racial backgrounds already, but I think that I became more conscious of using culturally relevant references. This means not talking about a person in a wheelchair who had a skiing accident when skiing isn't a sport to which most of the kids have access. It means not referring to TV shows and musical groups that Black kids don't watch or listen to. This means learning about what they do in their spare time, what they watch on television, what music they listen to, and what they read. This means listening to and forming an informed opinion about hip-hop and rap music rather than dismissing it as misogynist and violent work of drug dealing gangsters. Besides, I felt a whole lot more credible saying that I thought Tupac Shakur was smart and had some valuable stuff to say, but that I couldn't get past the language that Snoop Dogg used to describe women.

In short, I had to respect the students just as I would any other audience members. In some ways, I had to respect them more because I had so much more contact with them. I also became more acutely aware of the absolute need to have respect for an audience as a prerequisite to their being open to my message as a trainer. Sometimes, this was harder to do in corporations than with kids.

Working with the students at Weaver was about the most fun I've ever had. Where else was I going to learn things like Tupac Shakur's nickname was Machiavelli because he planned his own death? Or that his mother punished him by making him read the New York Times cover to cover as a child?

At Weaver, I learned about how people in general, not just teenagers, come to have an understanding about disability issues. I got to test out several assumptions that prior to this experience were theoretical. These assumptions had either occurred to me on my own or were part of an unwritten body of common wisdom about diversity training. Come to think of it, I'm sure that this wisdom had been written about somewhere; I just hadn't read it. Anyway, these are some of the theories that actually panned out.

Theory One: Multiple exposure is more effective than minimal exposure.

As my ten year old would say, "Duh." Some people instantly come to understand what you are trying to communicate. Some even know it before you talk to them; others may never get it. Still others—I hate to even think about how many since I tend to only get the opportunity to do single exposure training—require multiple exposure to the material. We'd always known that this was true of legal training and I had strongly suspected that this was the case with awareness training.

Moral of the story: Train people as much and as often as they will allow you to.

Theory Two: Multiple trainers are more effective than single trainers.

Again, "Duh." I brought in a variety of speakers with disabilities to classes that focused on awareness. I corralled anyone that I knew with a disability to come in to speak to classes. Some kids could relate to other speakers better than they related to me. Hearing the same message from different people with different disabilities helped them get it. Plus, they liked the opportunity to ask them all if and how they had sex.

Moral of the story: If given the opportunity to work with a group on numerous occasions, regularly coerce any friends and colleagues who are at all articulate about the issue and members of the oppressed group in question, to come and speak. Pay them if you must.

Theory Three: Left to their own devices, People Figure This Stuff Out By Themselves When Given the Opportunity.

When exposed to real live people with real live disabilities, the kids learned a lot more about disability issues and acted appropriately with very little coaching. I had secretly wondered about this theory. I'd given it lots of lip service, but I worried about trusting kids, or anyone else for that matter, to do the right thing. The bottom line is that the theory holds up, but we'll talk about that when we look at including kids with severe disabilities in regular classrooms.

There were some theories that didn't pan out, at least not for me. One is that if someone doesn't get it, this means that they haven't been exposed enough, the trainer hasn't presented it clearly or effectively enough, or they are not interested enough or intelligent enough to understand.

This theory is from the But-I'm-Right-And-They-Should-See-It school of diversity training. Or if you weren't so ableist, racist, sexist, or homophobic—fill in any applicable "ist" of your own—you'd agree with me. The reality is that some good-hearted people, even after a lot of exposure to training and/or people with disabilities, are still uncomfortable with us. I remember one of my most insightful students telling me that, yes, he had learned a lot in the classes that I taught, and that, yes, many of his misconceptions had been cleared up, but that he was still uncomfortable around people with disabilities. He hoped he'd never get one and he still felt sorry for people who did. I'm not sure that I can say that either of us failed.

Guest Speakers

I persuaded lots of people with different disabilities to come and talk to students in my social studies classes. The kids' responses were interesting, but not as fascinating as the speakers' responses to the students. It seems that for lots of adults, even those who are comfortable speaking in public, teenagers—particularly those who look different from them and go to a school that they've only heard about on the local news—represent the last frontier. New frontiers tend to be a bit scary. It wasn't that anyone came in and bombed, but I saw people who were normally very articulate become a little less so. I saw some people who are completely at ease testifying before Congress or running large organizations and businesses squirm just a little when asked a question by a fifteen-year-old.

It seemed that the speakers often learned as much as the kids. I remember having one speaker come in first period on the day after Christmas vacation. One of the students dragged himself through the door. My friend who was presenting that day commented that he seemed tired. Probably reminiscing about his own high school days, he asked the student if he'd spent the past week partying. The student replied, "No, sir. I had a baby over vacation."

The intriguing part was that I could rarely predict who would be a great speaker and who would be just okay. I remember being concerned about one woman who has a psychiatric disability and now works in state government. She was quite a bit older than the kids and for a whole lot of reasons didn't seem to have a whole lot in common with them. She was able to reach the kids in the class at a deeper level in one forty-two minute class than I was in an entire semester. Part of the reason for her success was that in addition to being a dynamic speaker, she was comfortable with them. She had once been a teacher in a Hartford elementary school. She was so comfortable that she was willing to probe just a little more than myself and the other speakers. When discussing an event, she could say, "It seems like you feel really sad/angry." For all these reasons the kids just opened up to her. Guest speakers can be good in that they keep you humble.

Guest speakers with disabilities weren't the only way that I got students to meet and hopefully connect with people with disabilities. Many of the students at Weaver are labeled as having disabilities. Most go to regular classes and get some support from special education staff. Another group of students spend most of their school day in the special education room. These were kids with severe disabilities even by my standards. All had some form of serious mental retardation. Most were non-verbal. In the case of one student, there was debate as to how much if anything he could see because he was cognitively unable to indicate vision. None walked or used a toilet independently.

The wonderful man who taught one of these classes was the person who responded to my Request for Proposal and was responsible for me being in the school. While I don't support educating kids—even ones with very severe disabilities—in separate classes, I have the utmost respect for Ted, their teacher.

One thing that I did with one of the first classes that I worked with was to give students the opportunity to spend time hanging out in the special education classroom. I tried to make it very clear that the regular education students who spent time in the special ed class were not doing community service, although they might be called upon to help out on occasion. If anyone was doing community service, it was the kids with disabilities who were sharing their classroom home and aspects of their life style as people with disabilities. I explained that there are many ways to teach. Some people did it by talking; other people could educate by showing someone how they live. This is what the special education students would be doing. I wanted students to leave the special ed class appreciating what they had learned, not that they had had spent the class "helping the handicapped." Believing that you are a purveyor of charity gets in the way of learning and certainly doesn't support you in adopting a rights-bearing attitude.

Some students didn't want to spend time with students in the special education room. That was fine. I didn't want anyone to be there who didn't want to. It wasn't fair to them or their hosts. Other kids went once or twice. Two girls asked their teacher to go back repeatedly. Their teacher allowed them to do this because, after almost thirty years of teaching, Faye had a good sense of when kids just wanted to get out of class and when they had other motivations. She wasn't exactly sure what their motives were but she let it go for a while.

Eventually, the two girls let it spill. They'd gotten to know and like one of the students in special education and they did not like how an aide was treating him when the teacher was out of the room. The social studies teacher, the special ed teacher and the girls met to discuss this. The special ed teacher surreptitiously watched the aide when he was out of the room and concurred with the girls. He didn't like how this student was being treated when he was out of the room, either. We're not talking about abuse or blatant neglect by the aide, but the student was not being treated as respectfully as he would have been had everyone been aware that the teacher was present. The aide was disciplined and her behavior changed.

These students successfully performed an intervention and advocated for their peer. They told the teacher that it was all right to share their story but they didn't want their names mentioned. My guess is that they were the two girls who beamed as she told it. This was an example of people instinctively doing the right thing without much, if any, prompting. Adults had probably been in the class without the teacher present. They may or may not have observed what the girls did. Possibly, the aides were more diligent in the presence of adults. I wonder, though, if it wasn't a little more complicated. The girls had no clinical or other training. But they had the expectation that people in the room would and should be treated with respect. Maybe they saw because they didn't have as much to unlearn as the professionals.

The girls had gotten to like the charming young man who they had advocated for so much that they nominated him to be honorary prom king. You can argue that it was too little way too late, but it was hard not to be moved when Carlos (not his real name) was crowned and danced in his wheelchair at his Senior Prom.

This was another humbling experience. Why waste my time training when I can achieve outcomes like that just by throwing people together? These kids might not have used politically correct language, but they clearly figured out everything that was important on their own. I guess the lesson in this for me as a trainer is that I should arrange this sort of thing whenever possible. Unfortunately, it is not always possible to do this in real life. Once again I saw that training, for all its potential benefits, is not the ideal.

In the following year of the project, I brought kids with disabilities who had been previously taught in a separate classroom into a regular one. This is called inclusion in education circles. Okay, it is often called many other less polite things by naysayers. For some reason that I can't say I fully understand, the idea of providing kids with disabilities an education in a regular classroom with their peers is controversial. In my experience, inclusion, when done right—that is, with sufficient support for classroom teachers—is a win-win.

But I'm not going to get into a philosophical discussion of inclusion here, although I believe that it is the best option for students with and without disabilities. I'm going to look at inclusion from the perspective of a diversity trainer. It wasn't until, I think, the third year of the grant that I proposed to do inclusion. An inclusion project initially would have been threatening to the school. They wouldn't want advocates marching into their school and telling them that they should be providing education in a radically different and often more costly way despite extremely limited resources. I disagree philosophically, but I certainly see their point. My major motivation for coming to the school was to promote a better understanding of the ADA and disability issues. Inclusion was not my primary mission. Later, it became apparent to me that inclusion was a natural way to do this. The result was a kind of guerilla inclusion.

In the middle of one spring semester, I began by including one girl with a severe disability into a social studies current events class. I'd been working with these kids since September, so I knew them rather well. I discussed with them the fact that we would be including a student from the special education class. The first question that they asked was what was her disability. This was fair, given that they had asked the same question of probably a dozen guest speakers. I explained that she used a wheelchair but beyond that I really didn't want to discuss her disability. It wasn't the same as if she were a guest speaker who had volunteered to come in and discuss her disability. At that point, the classroom teacher was on a medical leave and a student teacher was filling in. He relished the opportunity to do inclusion.

After I left that week, the kids kept repeating their questions about her disability to David, the student teacher. One thing that I've learned as a trainer is that when people repeat a question after you think you have answered the question, you probably haven't answered it. Or at least you haven't provided them with the information that they were seeking. After a couple of different kids asked what was "wrong" with this student and David patiently explained that having a disability did not mean that there was anything wrong with you, he asked them why they were so curious.

One of the kids finally asked if she was dangerous. David responded by saying, "Of course not." He was baffled as to why these kids, many of whom had seen an awful lot on the street, most of whom had personally known someone who had been shot, were threatened by this young woman. She was less than five feet tall, weighed under a hundred pounds and used a wheelchair. The kids assumed that there must be some reason that she was required to be alone only with kids with disabilities in the back of the school at the end of the hall for all these years. If she could be there without harming anyone, why wouldn't she have been part of their class a long time ago? Alas, these kids were assuming that this world is a lot more logical than it actually is.

Again, the kids came to the right conclusion, at least in part. Marisol (not her real name) belonged with them. Before Marisol came to class, I did an activity on the purposes of going to school. I asked the students to brainstorm about what of value had they learned in school. I forbade them to mention anything to do with academics. I asked, "What is it that you really learn here?" The first kid to speak called out that they learned to be consumers. "You know, Miss, you learned to buy and sell things," he said with a wink in his eye. I asked him to say more. He and others talked about how you learned what clothes to wear, how to talk, what music to listen to, and how to make friends at school. I asked them if they needed a high IQ or even the ability to read to learn these things or to benefit from knowing them. Obviously, the answer was, "No."

Then I asked how their lives would be different if they hadn't learned these things at school. What if the only people teaching them about this were parents and maybe teachers. What if your parents were the ones who taught you about clothes? Adolescent horror momentarily filled the room. That is why it is important for everyone, regardless of ability, to be with their peers, I explained. You learn about many things other than academics in school. They seemed to get it. For the rest of the semester, Marisol became just another member of the class.

I was simultaneously doing inclusion in one of the tech preparation classes. In the class, the students were learning the basics of accessible design. We used the school as a laboratory. We would survey the school for architectural barriers and the students would be assigned to develop solutions. Ostensibly, because I wasn't using my wheelchair a lot that term, I asked a couple of the kids in special ed to conduct surveys with us. By virtue of the fact that they used wheelchairs, they would demonstrate first hand why building codes were written the way they are. A kid who can't approach the sink because there is not enough knee clearance under a sink drives home this point much more powerfully than any lecture on wheelchair access. Once again, the special ed kids were in a valued role as instructor. They were assisting the kids without disabilities, not vice-versa.

Although I did some awareness work with the tech prep students, I mostly focused on facility accessibility with them. We toured the school and local businesses—I like to think that I've spent more time in the boys' bathroom than any other woman in history. Realizing the number of places people with disabilities cannot go is inherently a consciousness raising experience. Being with another student who can't use the school bathrooms or visit the local grocery store because of structural barriers brings the lesson home deeply.

Inevitably, the students began to ask "Why?" Given that there were laws requiring barrier removal and given the one that applied to schools had been in effect for nearly twenty years, they wanted to know why illegal barriers existed. I reminded them that the Civil Rights Act had been passed in 1964, long before any of them were born and I asked them if racial discrimination still happened. They got it.

Later, the teacher included a student with severe mental retardation and cerebral palsy in his class. One of the class projects was for students to design a wheelchair accessible house. While James couldn't articulate his preferences, he could make choices given two options. He was thrilled when he saw his design emerge from the printer.

During this semester, I arranged a couple of group activities for the social studies current issues class, the tech prep class (both of which had included students with disabilities) and students in the special ed class who had not yet been included in regular classes. First, we had a pizza party.

Training Tip: The way to an audience's heart, especially a teenage audience's heart, is through their stomachs. An audience with elevated blood sugar is a happy audience.

At the pizza party, I did a few activities designed to force people to talk to each other. In one, the students were asked to find the individual in the room who had the birthday closest to their own. Kids who were unable to speak because of their disability had a card on the tray of their wheelchair with their birthday written on it. The pair with the closest birthday got a gift certificate for ice cream. Again, I capitalized on teenagers' perpetually empty stomachs.

Having kids spend even very short periods of time together is an effective way to promote comfort with diversity. Trainers should do this whenever they can. Sometimes the simplest solutions elude us.

I don't want to sound glib. It isn't always as simple as putting kids with disabilities with non-disabled kids together. The cliché that kids can be cruel is a cliché for a reason. The harassment of kids with disabilities is a huge problem. I've talked to a number of teenagers with disabilities who prefer a less than adequate school just for kids with disabilities to an integrated school where peers are insensitive. It is true that separate is never equal but sometimes it is more kind.

I learned a lot about race and racism at Weaver. For the most part, working with students who experience discrimination on a regular basis made communicating the concept of ableism easier. The first time I talked to the kids about race and disability was interesting. Picture the scene. I was brand new to the school and had spoken to maybe one other group there—I think that was the honor society. (By the way, the honor society was exactly like honor societies I had visited in the more affluent suburbs. The only time I truly captured their attention was when I mentioned that I had a law degree. They wanted to know about where I went to school and what my law school entrance test scores were.)

This class was for students who, without getting clinical, were basically labeled *difficult*. When I arrive, I'm greeted by a woman who introduces herself as a substitute teacher. She asks if I still want to do this. I tell her that I'm here anyway, so why not go ahead. Besides, I'll be damned if I'll run away. Kids and wild animals sense fear and I wasn't going to buy in. Then another woman comes in and introduces herself as the teacher in the class next door. She knows that there is a substitute and that I'm a guest speaker; she asks if I still want to do this. "Yes," I say. Okay, I admit that by this time I'm getting a little nervous. Then she asks if it is all right with me if she comes into the class if she hears loud voices. "Sure," I say, "the more the merrier." At this point I was starting to feel like Michelle Pfeiffer at the beginning of the movie Dangerous Minds. So, about a half dozen kids come in—five boys and one girl, as I recall. They made it clear that they didn't want to pay any attention to me. They were talking and reading magazines—sneaking peeks at pictures in National Geographic (I swear). So much for the worldly street bravado.

I decided to use the thirty seconds of advice that the teacher in the other classroom had given me. After all, she seemed like she had obviously lived through the experience and I didn't know what the hell else to do. The crux of what she said was to divide and conquer, never address the whole group. Pick one kid and talk to him. Tell him that you demand respect. This more or less worked. Who knows, maybe they were curious about what I had to say.

I talked about why I was there and about the ADA and how it was an anti-discrimination law for people with disabilities. One of the kids finally said, "Slow down, Miss. We can't understand what you are saying." (My Federal Express commercial delivery is exacerbated by stress.) Another student joked that I was almost rapping it. Then he said, "You know, you say you people are discriminated against. It's not nearly as bad as us." Normally, I won't get into a discussion of comparative oppression. But what came out of my mouth was, "What's the unemployment rate for African Americans? For people with disabilities it is around 75 percent. That means that one in four of us that are able to work are working." At this point he said, "So what do you do? How do you ever get a job?" I said, "You just go in and convince an employer that you'll be ten times as good as a non-disabled employee. Then you have to be ten times as good when they hire you. Sound familiar?" They got it.

This, of course, wasn't the only context in which racism as compared to ableism came up. In the past, when I'd trained staff of non-profit organizations, people of color particularly resonated with the idea that disability was a civil rights issue and that the ADA was civil rights law. I assumed that this would also be the case at Weaver. It wasn't, at least not for everyone. I became aware of this one day when I overheard two African American teachers talking. One of the women had gone to her daughter's graduation from an Ivy League college the previous weekend. Gloria Steinem gave the commencement address. The teacher was horrified that Gloria Steinem had characterized women's rights as a civil rights issue. Okay, I was going to have to think about how I presented this to students.

I'm a firm believer that you can get people to forgive, if not believe, anything if you preface it enough, so that's how I dealt with presenting disability rights as a civil rights issue. I told students that I was not intending to say that the discrimination experienced by people with disabilities was worse than or even the same as that experienced by African Americans, but that there are some parallels. Besides that, the ADA legally is a civil rights law. The statute itself describes people with disabilities as a protected class who have historically been discriminated against.

I focused on the double impact of disability for African Americans. First, African Americans are more likely to acquire a disability. This is due in part to inferior health care and to the greater likelihood of being poor and living in more violent high crime environments. Second, discrimination experienced on the basis of race is compounded by disability. People of color with disabilities are more likely to be unemployed than are white people with disabilities. When they are employed, they earn less than white people with disabilities. I reminded students not to fall into the trap of fighting with each other over pieces of an inadequate pie when what was needed was a pie large enough to serve everyone. Participants, whether they are students or adults, are more able to hear and appreciate a message when presented like this, than a message that says or can be interpreted to say "We have it worse than you."

It was an oversimplification—a racist oversimplification—for me to characterize students at Weaver as African American. Although I intellectually knew that roughly forty per cent of the students were from Jamaica, it took a while for this to register. I looked into a room and saw people with varying shades of brown skin. I had no appreciation for the fact that I was interacting with kids from vastly different cultures and the impact that this would have in developing and presenting training.

The students from Jamaica didn't have as much of a Civil Rights orientation. Their parents and grandparents had not been part of the Civil Rights movement. Many of them learned about the civil rights movement for the first time in their high school social studies class. This was actually true for some of the African American students as well. Their overall attitude was less of a rights-baring one.

The Jamaican students were generally more conservative. They were more likely to be the students who wrote essays about why pregnant girls should not be allowed to go to school, whereas the African American kids were more likely to have children of their own. Of course, I'm speaking in broad generalizations and there were many exceptions, but what was important is that these two groups of kids had radically different life experiences, often until very recently. At minimum, they were products of vastly different educational systems. Jamaican students wore uniforms, spent more time in class and had a generally stricter environment. I remember when the kids first found out that their new principal was Jamaican; all of the students in the class, including the Jamaican ones, groaned. I asked what their problem was with this person who they hadn't met yet. They said, "Miss, she's Jamaican. That means she's strict."

There were also racial tensions between groups of African American students and Jamaican students. Before I went to Weaver, I had associated racial tension with starkly obvious differences in skin tone. I also thought that brown skin, at least in the same geographic region, meant one culture. I rarely considered different shades of brown or different accents. Just shows what I knew. Obviously, I needed to keep all of this in mind as I provided training.

Training Tip: Know who your audience is.

Moral of the story: I'm just as racist as your average white liberal.

Aside from cultural differences, skin tone was an issue within groups of Jamaican and African American students. I remember one day, after an access survey field trip, that one of the boys was flirting with one of the girls. When he left I said to the girl, "He's pretty cute. What do you think?" She said, "He's too dark for me." I have to admit to being taken aback. It wasn't that I was unaware of this phenomenon. It just looked different in real life than it had in a diversity training classroom.

The experience of providing training to the kids at Weaver was really not fundamentally different than providing training to adults. The kids dressed differently, talked differently and to some degree had a different set of behaviors, but the primary experience was virtually indistinguishable. Some participants were incredibly engaged and got a lot out of training. Some didn't. Some were bored and resentful. Kind of like every other adult audience. The same participant types that had followed me from training to training were there. Except that at Weaver the acting out adolescents actually were teenagers.

Social cues were different, though. In one class, there was a student who sat at the back of the class with his head down on his desk for the entire semester. I wouldn't have recognized him in the hall because I had never seen his face. As a parent, and now as a trainer/teacher type, I had learned to pick my battles. At least by being silent he wasn't disrupting the class. This kid was lost and it was a waste of my time to even try. So, I basically ignored him.

In retrospect, it should have dawned on me that his veteran no-nonsense teacher probably would not have put up with this behavior if there wasn't more to it. In spite of this kid, we had a great semester. On the day before Christmas Break, I came armed with candy and other treats. I gave candy to students who correctly answered questions on material that I had been covering since September. Guess who knew the answers to most of my questions? The kid who, prior to this, had never shown his face. I didn't hear another word from him again until I brought candy in the spring. At the end of the course, he thanked me, shook my hand and said how much he had liked the program.

Moral of this story: When learning, people do not all look or act alike.

Redundant moral: If you have doubt about whether or not you are reaching someone, ask.

Also: What they say about assuming is true.

Some of the most insightful comments and questions came from the kids at Weaver. This is not to say that they didn't ask not-so-insightful questions on a regular basis, too. I know, there is no such thing as a stupid question. But after the eighth person that day asks you if you have snow tires for that thing, referring to your wheelchair, you begin to wonder. One student in particular asked the most interesting questions. I called him the vice president in charge of questions and called on him whenever things got slow with a guest speaker. He asked one of the speakers who was born blind to describe her dreams. To another presenter who had no physical ability to speak, but communicated through use of a speech synthesizer and a communication board he said, "You don't talk, right?" The speaker nodded. "You never have?" Again he nodded. The student then said, "When I think, I hear a voice in my head. What about you?" I was impressed. He also wasn't shy about saying the things that other participants, both adults and kids, were reluctant to say. He would diplomatically ask (to the degree that you can be diplomatic in asking this question) how people with disabilities could stand their lives given their physical condition and the reality of the discrimination that they faced. Questions like this opened the door for speakers to truly communicate the realities, both negative and positive, of their lives.

During my final semester at Weaver, before I took a maternity leave, I had the opportunity to submit a proposal to a national conference on disability rights and education. The conference happened to be held in Boston that year, about a two-hour drive from Hartford. Rather than presenting myself, I invited the students to come to Boston and do the presentation. Aside from being a logistical nightmare, it was a great experience. First, I had to get the people at the organization sponsoring the conference to agree to let us come. That wasn't too much of a problem. My next task was to get the administration to allow the students and chaperoning teachers to go. They were fine with students going, but there was resistance to hiring a substitute for one of the teachers. This wouldn't have been a big deal except that we had to have two teachers present in order to be able to go. As a civilian, I didn't count.

Eventually, we got permission for the teachers and the students to go. One of the teachers wrote a grant or somehow finagled enough money from his teachers association to pay for a bus. We arranged for a personal assistant for one of the students with a disability and, yes, someone made sure that the bus had a lift. Kids brought in signed permission slips; getting these adolescents to do this was not unlike pulling teeth, but somehow it happened.

We had our bus. We had our kids. We had our staff. The night before the presentation, it snowed. Did I mention that the conference was being held in New England in the middle of December? I was in Boston doing another training and panicking. I talked to one of the teachers the night before the conference. Things looked doubtful. If either school was canceled or the bus company thought it was dangerous, the kids couldn't come. The weather in Hartford was predicted to be worse than it was in Boston. Sometimes, the superintendent cancelled school at the drop of a hat. She didn't this time. Only a dozen or so of the twenty students who had signed up made the early morning bus. One of the students who didn't make it was Marisol, the young woman who had been included in the social studies class. But thirteen students made it.

I was just a little nervous. Kids were missing, we hadn't rehearsed enough and I was just coming off a relatively unsuccessful experience of training adults to be trainers. So here I was with a group of kids, a couple of whom I didn't know well because they had gotten involved at the last minute, about to speak before a national audience. Hey, if I really cared about my professional reputation I wouldn't have tried most of the things that I did in training. Still, these kids were in a strange city, in a grand ballroom of a hotel; they had to be terrified. We were all way too cool to admit it, though.

I had asked one of the tech prep kids to talk about disability as a civil rights issue. In retrospect, that was odd, because we'd spent very little time discussing that in his class and a lot of time on it in the social studies class. But he seemed to get it and for some reason I trusted him. After I did a brief introduction describing how the project was funded and other boring details, I let the kids take over.

When he started by saying "Jim Crow Laws are alive and well for people with disabilities in the United States," I wanted to cry. This kid had really gotten it. The rest of the students did equally well. They talked about access and demonstrated how to conduct a mini access survey; they discussed stereotypes of people with disabilities in the media; they talked about inclusion of people with severe disabilities in their classes. I should be so eloquent.

After the presentation, several participants offered us money to all go out to lunch. I told the kids that no one had ever offered to pay for my lunch after a training. We thanked them, but explained that we had planned for that.

I feel like I should be able to offer an explanation as to why this went so well, but I don't have one. Not when I'd seen adults with a lot more experience, education and privilege bomb under my humble tutelage. The phrase "through no fault of my own" comes to mind.

TRAINING ACTIVITY: EVERYBODY KNOWS

Everybody Knows isn't so much an activity as a gimmick. Did I ever say that there was anything wrong with using gimmicks in a training? Like Fabulous Prizes, gimmicks are vaguely amusing. Unlike Fabulous Prizes, they have a point that is relevant to the training. What I do in this particular gimmick is to write *Everybody Knows* on a piece of newsprint. I then draw a circle around it. Then I draw a red bar through the circle. I tell the group that the next time they say or they hear someone say "everybody knows," they should question it. I ask them to take a look at all the "everybody knowses" that have been proven untrue just in the little while that we have been together. Everybody knows that you can't work if you can't even sit up. Everybody knows that professionals know best...

TRAINING ACTIVITY: SCREW DRIVER/ WHEELCHAIR

While I'm on gimmicks, I might as well tell you about this one, too. Sometimes when I'm bored in a training or I want to bring a little extra energy into a room, I do this quick activity.

Training Hint: If as a trainer you are bored, chances are that intractable ennui is setting into the room like gangrene. You better wake up and do something immediately to liven up the room so they don't forever associate diversity training with existential dread.

Anyhow, what I do is bring out a screw driver and a toy wheelchair or sometimes I just motion to my own wheelchair, should I happen to be using it, and ask what these two things have in common. Sometimes they struggle with it. Sometimes they get it right away. The answer: both are tools.

After this, we discuss that a wheelchair is merely a tool. Unfortunately, lots of people see it as a symbol of infirmity, incompetence and dependence. Or as I say to young kids, "We think that wheelchairs are sad things when really they are happy ones." One of the high school students told me that in her culture sitting in a wheelchair, say in a hospital waiting room, was considered tempting fate and never should be done. As an overeducated white person, I could dismiss this as superstition from a more primitive culture. But I notice that lots of my fellow overeducated white friends are hesitant to sit in vacant wheel chairs in my living room when we've run out of regular chairs. It seems that a lot of the time *primitive* actually means candid.

We've all been taught that wheelchairs are depressing and that the people who use them are perpetually depressed and longing for a cure. This makes sense when given that they are incompetent, dependent and otherwise miserable.

Some of the best efforts to change the perception of the wheelchair as a negative symbol have been geared toward children. This is good, considering that childhood is when most of us learned this. One recent effort is the relatively famous Barbie doll who uses a wheelchair. I'm not a great fan of Barbie as a role model for little girls. She encourages unrealistic body expectations and frivolous consumerism. Okay, I had them as a child and as an adult I've collected a few myself, but that doesn't mean that I approve. But the idea of an attractive doll that uses a wheelchair is compelling, even if she is politically incorrect.

My favorite example of an effort to de-stigmatize wheelchairs is also one of my favorite books. It is called *Mama Zooms* by Jane Cowen-Fletcher (1993 Scholastic Inc.). *Mama Zooms* is written from the perspective of a toddler whose Mama happens to use a wheelchair. The little boy and his Mama zoom through life pretending that the wheelchair is a train, a plane, a wave in the ocean or a bunch of other exciting things. It is the first book that I have seen that suggests that not only is it okay to use a wheelchair, but that a wheelchair is pretty cool.

5

Audiences—The Good, the Bad and the Usually Not Too Ugly

This chapter is devoted to audiences who, contrary to the opinion of most trainers, are the actual stars of any training. Without them, trainers would just be shouting their message into the air. It is upon audiences that good trainers work their magic.

One of the best things about training is that you get to share your thoughts and ideas with a group of strangers and find out what they think. Even better, sometimes you can persuade them that what you are saying has merit and that they should listen. The best of all is when people change as a result of something you have said. That is when training goes from a meeting with trainer standing in front of a room with her stories and gimmicks and devices to a place where magic happens. Good training isn't simply about instilling information or even inculcating values; it is about transformation. This is true whether the training is about attitudes or about the law. In either case, during the best trainings, at least some of the participants leave the room changed from when they came in. They see the world differently. They see themselves differently and they see people with disabilities and their relationship to them differently.

Characters Who Come to a Training

Much like the archetypal characters that seemed to have followed me around all my life and that I made into masks, there are characters who repeatedly come to my trainings. It's not just me, really; other people have noticed this as well, and have even written about it. They show up at most trainings. They are different genders, different ages and hold a variety of jobs. But their behavior and message are strikingly similar. Let's take a look at a few of these participants.

The Cheerleader

The cheerleader is a great participant. She is a pleasure to have in any training. She makes your job easy. She agrees with everything you say and shows this by nodding vigorously throughout the training. She'll defend you to the death if other group members question your material or style. I find myself wishing that all participants could be cheerleaders. Then I have to remind myself that she's not the reason that I'm there. The cheerleader has gotten it already. She doesn't need me. Still, it wouldn't be bad to have an entire audience of cheerleaders…maybe just once.

The Wannabe

Like the cheerleader, the Wannabe gets the issues almost instinctively. The problem is that she understands them better than you do. In every way. All of the time. Not only does she have a better grasp of the law or the issues, she would be better at presenting them than you are. She reminds you of this during breaks, in evaluations, and sometimes in front of the group. Her criticisms range from questions about the accuracy of the content you are presenting to the arrangement of the furniture in the room. Sadly, Wannabe's are often fellow diversity trainers. They may not be deliberately getting in their own way of absorbing material. It's just hard not to evaluate minor details when you do this type of work for a living.

I have to work hard not to be a Wannabe when I go to other people's trainings. Nothing frustrates me more than people who I perceive as not having a grasp on the material. Note that the emphasis here is on the phrase "I perceive." I need to watch out that I don't hastily jump to conclusions.

I find that the best way to handle Wannabes is to make friends with them. Acknowledge them. Respect their expertise. Include them if you can. Depending on the circumstances, they may be threatened by your presence. This is how one trainer managed a Wannabe (me) that was in her audience. I wasn't being an overt Wannabe during the training. Really I wasn't. (Rare is the Wannabe who totally cops to it.) But this poor woman had me for a five-day training. During dinner on the first night, we got talking about what we did in real life. I must have Wannabeed at her. She asked me if I would train with her because in certain areas I had more experience.

Hint: If someone asks you to train with them spontaneously, you have probably Wannabeed just a little.

Another tactic is to ignore Wannabes. In one ADA training, I had a participant read the regulation to himself as I presented and he almost joyfully called out whenever I didn't state the regulation exactly. This person wasn't a trainer and I never did find out what was up with him. Each time he interrupted, I thanked him and explained that my intention was not to quote the regulation, but to explain and summarize it. What I really wanted to do was to quote my ten year old and say, "Whatever." But why should I get all worked up because someone else, for whatever reason, is threatened and needs to be right? It doesn't diminish me, my training or the benefits that participants get from a training. Ah, detachment…when you can actually pull it off, it can be a wonderful thing.

The Should Be Wannabe

Should Be Wannabes are people that have ten thousand times more experience, information and expertise than you do and have ended up in your training for God knows what reason. They have the gall to be humble and not bring attention to your lack of expertise. You might not even know that they have been there until after the training. My favorite experience with Should Bes was during my very first long ADA training. There were two of them. Both were attorneys. One was a special education expert who had been litigating disability rights cases and drafting federal special education policy forever. The second had just published a 600-page tome on the employment provisions of the ADA on which, by the way, I would be training for the first time. Fortunately, someone gave me the heads up immediately before the training. I spoke to each of them briefly and encouraged them to jump right in if I got something wrong. I also introduced them to the audience and explained that they were the true experts in the room. They could not have been more gracious. I could not have been more intimidated.

The Acting—Out Adolescent

First, let me say that many of my favorite people in the universe are teenagers. Given the choice between training an audience of adults at random and an audience of teenagers at random, I would choose teenagers. Characterizing difficult participants as teenagers is not intended to be a slight, but a cheap exploitation of a common stereotype. Seriously, the characteristics I am about to describe would be more developmentally appropriate in an adolescent than in an adult; hence, I have labeled it as such.

The acting-out adolescent audience member can take on many forms. S/he may be sullen and withdrawn. His or her facial expression and body language may communicate the height of boredom. S/he knows it all already, didn't care to begin with and has much more important things to be doing with his or her time. When the expression of boredom is accompanied by eye rolling, it's a bit like training Mick Jagger. As a trainer, you have a choice to ignore these people or win them over. I almost always at least attempt to do the latter.

The Acting-Out Adolescent who I just described is easier to deal with than the next version. This character acts out and is disruptive. He doesn't want to be there. He shouldn't have to be there. You can make him go, but you can't make him listen. I have a couple of extreme examples of this type of participant.

One came to a two-day training presented by a friend of mine. Fortunately I only had to present a one-hour module. Some audience members were angry because they had heard that my friend was going to criticize how people with mental retardation were treated in group homes and other facilities run by the state. They didn't want to go to the training, but their supervisors required that they attend. So, these state employees came. They sat in the front row. They put cotton in their ears. I swear to God that this actually happened.

Training Hint: If you have any say whatsoever and you don't want audience members to stuff foreign objects in their ears, avoid mandatory training.

Lest state employees feel that they've been singled out, I will share a tale of one extreme corporate Acting-Out Adolescent. I suspected that I had a problem when this guy started making fun of the fact that we had asked participants to wear name tags. During the training, he squirmed, refused to make any eye contact and basically insulted us. Not many people tried to get him to shut up because, as luck or something would have it, he was the CEO. Just as other adolescents may follow when one acts out, so followed some of the adults. The best part was when this guy deliberately dropped trash on the floor to see who would pick it up. No one did. I'm still not sure why he paid us to be there; he claimed that he had misunderstood what we would be talking about.

The good part—okay, I am overly optimistic sometimes—was that the behavior was so outrageous that even I couldn't find a way to beat myself up about it. I couldn't say, "If only I had thought to say…" or "So and so, trainer extraordinaire, would have done a better job." No one was going to be able to reach this guy. As we were leaving, my training partner—we were working together for the first time, by the way—said, "My, that was heinous." I agreed, invited her out to lunch and forgot about it.

These are just a few of the characters that I regularly encounter in trainings. Of course they represent extremes.

What "Getting It" Can Look Like

What does it mean for participants to "get it"? More importantly, what does it look like when they do? Lots of the time, participants go through a training nodding and seeming to get most of what you say as soon as you say it. Other people never get it or at least don't get it while they are still in the training room.

The really fun participants are the ones who don't get it at first, but visibly come to understand and embrace your message at some point during the training experience. A couple of people come to mind. One woman at a training in Texas had been quiet for most of a three-day ADA training. Then, midway through the last day, she got this look of understanding and said, "So, it's fair." The remark was kind of out of context. I asked what was fair and she said the ADA. I asked the rest of the group if they had heard what she had said and jokingly told them they could all go home. They had learned what I had come to teach them.

Another man sat through most of a daylong ADA/awareness training with his arms folded and generally looking hostile. Around 11:00 I decided that I had to know what was going on. I said, "You look as if there's something that you want to say." He looked a little startled because he hadn't raised his hand, but he took a breath and said, "I just don't understand why we are supposed to give people with disabilities special treatment." He didn't seem particularly angry anymore. I thought about how to respond. I said, "Look, if you want to go to city hall, you use the stairs. If I want to go to city hall, I use a ramp to get to the same place. It's not special treatment, but different ways of getting the same thing." This probably wasn't the most cogent explanation that I'd ever given, but I saw the light bulb go on. He understood. He made a point of sitting with me at lunch.

That man with his genuine candor gave the group and me an important gift. He was willing to take the risk of appearing ignorant or ableist or callous or whatever he feared people would see it as and admitted to not getting it. By taking that risk in front of his supervisors, he got an explanation that made sense to him and to the rest of the group. I used to avoid direct confrontation of participants who seemed to have problems with what I'm saying. I've come to encourage and embrace it.

When someone comes to understand in a way that they previously did not, the energy of the whole room changes. Other people get it, too. Sometimes the entire group visibly relaxes. I got to see this very graphically once while I was training a corporate audience. The company had just hired about a half dozen people who happened to be blind. They had not yet begun working and I was there to do what they called sensitivity training for a number of their future co-workers and supervisors. The group was welcoming, but there was a subtle current of tension in the air. Not always being very quick it took me a while to get a handle on exactly who had problems and what they were. I threw out a few trial balloons to see if any one would provide some insight. Even though I hadn't been hired to present ADA training, I matter-of-factly mentioned some of the requirements and, more important, non-requirements of the ADA. I told them that, yes, you did have to provide reasonable accommodations to people with visual disabilities but that, of course, after an employer did this they could and should hold these employees to the same performance standard as everyone else.

At that point, someone raised her hand and said, "Did you just say that after we provide equipment necessary for reasonable accommodation and allow for a reasonable training period, we can require blind employees to meet the same production standard as employees without disabilities?"

Training Hint: When someone repeats what you have just said in the form of a question, they have either been sleeping or are, one way or another, really excited about what you just said.

When I said "You got it" in response to her question, the room heaved a collective sigh of relief. Supervisors were worried about lower overall productivity and a decline in employee moral. Co-workers were worried about having to compensate for these employees who they hadn't even met yet. I was glad that this concern came up because ain't nobody in the room was going to get more comfortable with people with disabilities or learn about guide dogs or the technology that they would be using as long as they felt that their professional well-being was potentially being compromised.

Some people don't get it right away and need to be exposed to the concept repeatedly in various ways over a period of time. This speaks to the limit of one- or two-shot training opportunities. Other people don't get it even then. Maybe in time and with more exposure they will.

TRAINING ACTIVITY: THEM AND US

An activity that I developed very early on was one that I call Them and Us. This one I didn't lift from anyone, which is maybe why it took such a long time to work the kinks out of it. In Them and Us I use dolls. I got a certain amount of flak from my colleagues when I shared the idea of using dolls in an adult training. They correctly pointed out that it might be a bad idea to use dolls in a training when I was trying to teach participants to view people with disabilities as competent adults. How could I say "Don't be condescending to people with disabilities" if I was using dolls as props? How could I expect to be taken seriously? As with the Masks, I chose to ignore the common wisdom as I explored ways of keeping my professional ego intact while making a fool of myself. As with the Masks, audiences gave this activity higher ratings as I grew in confidence.

For Them and Us I bought a set of multi-racial, nine-inch, doll-house sized dolls, some of which had leg braces, crutches, white canes or wheelchairs. I would preface the activity by asking the group if they had ever felt any twinge of discomfort when they encountered a person with a disability. Had they ever felt like someone with a disability was more one of "them" than one of "us"? Then, I would hold up a doll that used a wheelchair. I would ask for a show of hands to determine whether or not the doll felt like a "them" or an "us." I would drop the doll into a plastic box labeled *them* or *us* according to the vote. I'd then hold up the same doll and tell participants that as they passed this guy on the street, he called them by name. As they looked at him, they realized that they had gone to school with him and hadn't seen him in at least five years. He explained that he had broken his leg in a car accident and would be laid up in this stupid chair another two months. I then re-poll the group. In almost every case, if the doll was a "them" before he becomes an "us" now. I move the doll to what is now the appropriate box.

I repeat this process with a blind doll that at first is a stranger and then becomes a favorite aunt. Again, with familiarity, the doll almost always moves to the *us* box.

I think that the most interesting part of this activity is when I hold up a doll without a disability and ask participants to imagine that she is wearing ragged clothes and carrying her possessions in a shopping cart. She mutters and rants to herself and to some people no one else can see. Even the most self-conscious, politically correct audience will vote that she is a "them." I then hold up another doll with no visible disability. She is dressed more like members of the group. She comes from the same social class as they do. This isn't surprising because she is their sister-in-law. She's kind of known as the family eccentric. They've heard that she takes medication for her nerves. Last Thanksgiving, they caught her when she thought she was alone talking and ranting to no one in particular. Is she one of "them" or one of "us"? Usually, she becomes one of "us."

I ask audiences to notice the movement of most of the dolls from the *them* box to the *us* box. I ask them what changed that compelled this movement. Typically, they talk about familiarity and comfort. Finally, I ask them who changed. Inevitably, they realize that it wasn't the physical or emotional or cognitive ability of the doll that changed. It was them.

A couple of things about this activity work well. I like the feeling of the movement of the dolls from the *them* box to the *us* box. It suggests that attitudes are fluid rather than fixed. Them and Us illustrates that it is not necessarily the disability of the doll per se that makes participants uncomfortable, but other factors such as class and familiarity that come into play. This opens up the idea that maybe they can change and become more comfortable with disabilities that they find alienating.

Them and Us clarifies that the context of the disability is as important if not more important than the disability itself in determining a participant's comfort level. We do better with disabilities when they are temporary, occur in people that we know, and that belong to people who are of our same social class. When time allows, I discuss saliva. I ask if people find adult drooling gross. Most say that they do. I ask if they are equally disgusted by a baby who drools. Few are. Again it is not the saliva per se that is offensive, but saliva in the "wrong" or unexpected context.

6

About Trainers

Where Do Good Trainers Come From Anyway?

The experience at Weaver brings up the question: "How do you get people to be able to do this training thing anyway?" I'm really not sure. Sometimes so-called training-of-trainer programs work, but often they don't. I've presented two types of training of trainer programs. The first is informational. Typically, this has been an optional final section of an ADA training. I've had them last from a couple of hours to one day to half- day sessions every few weeks over a period of several months. In this type of training my co-presenters and I are helping participants hone details of the law and methods of communicating it. The most challenging part of this type of program is getting participants to master the law. Typically, these are people with lots of other things on their plate, so getting them to commit the necessary time is difficult.

The second type of training prepares participants to be disability awareness or diversity trainers. This works best when participants come into the program with a relatively high degree of experience and/or natural ability. Training works best when participants have some sense of their own training style and aren't consciously or unconsciously trying to mimic the style of the trainers.

There are other characteristics that I look for in a trainer. One of the most important is that they have a disability. This is not to say that you can't be a great disability awareness trainer if you don't have a disability, but in the training-of-trainer sessions I conduct, I require non-disabled trainers to present with someone who has a disability. Just as I wouldn't presume to do racial diversity training alone as a white person, I don't think that it is appropriate for people without disabilities to present awareness training by themselves. Notice that I said awareness/diversity training, not legal training. As far as I'm concerned, there are two prerequisites for ADA and other disability rights law trainers. The first and most important one is that they have a command of the law. Second, they should be dynamic speakers who are able to engage an audience with ease.

A common mistake that organizations, as well as people with disabilities who hold themselves out as trainers, make is to assume that having a disability is by itself sufficient qualification to be a trainer. Beyond the obvious need for presentation skills, trainers must be able to develop material or be able to tailor existing material to a given audience. Trainers must have a degree of perspective. They have gotten past the stage of needing to tell their personal story so that they are able to be there for the purpose of enlightening an audience rather than telling their story.

Unless they are members of a panel where their job is to discuss their particular disability, they must understand some of the barriers experienced by people with disabilities other than their own. Like I said before, the presence of one disability doesn't automatically mean tolerance or understanding of another.

I've come to the conclusion that the best way for people to learn how to become awareness/diversity trainers is through apprenticeship. At least that is how I've been most successful. In an apprenticeship program, an individual typically shadows a trainer for an extended period of time gradually presenting modules with trainer supervision and feedback until she can present the entire training by herself.

Mine, Yours and Ours: Trainer Configurations

There are an infinite number of ways to present training. One of the first things that a trainer must decide is: Do I want to do it alone or with others? If you do it with others you'll have to work out a number of things, such as roles, etc. (See "Rules for Training With Partners..." later on in this chapter.) If you want to do it alone, you'll have to figure out what you'll do if and when you get into the variety of tight situations that inevitably arise.

At first, I dreaded the thought of training with a partner, much less a team. After all, this person would be evaluating each and every word I said, perhaps every gesture I made (this has happened more than once, so don't call me paranoid), and evaluating its accuracy, its relevance and its effectiveness. What if they knew more than I did? Wasn't I hard enough on myself without another professional critiquing me? I had barely gotten to the point where I could deal with audience feedback. Worse than that, what if they knew less than I did and got material or facts wrong?

Like it or not, I came to see training in teams and with partners as a necessary evil. If possible, no audience should be subjected to a single trainer for more than three hours. So if you want to provide a legal or awareness training that is more than introductory, you have to work with other trainers. After a short period of time, I discovered that working with others was a blessing that saved my sanity, my stamina and my sense of humor on a regular basis.

Initially, I felt exposed by having another trainer present. Then I had a revelation that I'll share. Whenever you get up in front of a bunch of people for many hours and share intimate details about your life experience or even try to impart some modest understanding of the law, you are exposed already. I got a glimmer of this truth when a training participant wrote on an evaluation that the robin's egg blue suit that I wore on the previous day worked much better with my complexion than the peach suit I had worn that day. She was right and I guess meant well. To this day, I think of her every time I wear the peach suit.

You are not more exposed by having another human being in the room who knows as much as you do. If anything, you are protected by this person. If your goal is to be accurate rather than to protect your ego, it can be important to have someone knowledgeable there. We all make mistakes. One time I had just come off a long run of training businesses in architectural obligations under the ADA. On this particular day, I was training staff from a state agency. I inadvertently told them the requirement for elevators in private businesses rather than the one for state facilities. I never would have noticed and neither would they. Out of the corner of my eye I saw my training partner semi-furiously flipping through an ADA manual. This is almost always a bad sign. At first, he wondered if he was crazy. I exuded confidence and clarity. It is important to present with utter confidence even if you are flat out wrong. He wasn't crazy and I wasn't right. So, he marked a passage in the book that stated the facts correctly and discretely made me aware of it.

Having been made aware of my mistake, I had two choices. I could ignore it, which really wasn't an option, or I could tell the truth. Okay, so I had one choice. The only real decision that I had to make was how to present this to the group. I stopped mid-thought and said to the group, "Guys, I just lied to you. Actually, I didn't lie. I screwed up. I just told you the completely wrong standard for elevators in state buildings." I proceeded to tell them why. Having a sense of humor is mandatory to a trainer's survival. It is also disarming. My training partner, a close friend, never again had any sense of trepidation about telling me about any mistakes I had made.

Co-trainers can emotionally rescue during a training should the need arise. Once in a training-of-trainers session, this very sweet older lady began to exhibit, as they say, challenging behavior. She began by criticizing people in the local and national disability rights movement. Not being willing to cast the first stone, I ignored this. It got a little strange when she demanded that we confront one of them about a weight problem. She then described how she wished her disabled daughter had been successful in her suicide attempt. Okay, we were now in the territory of impermissible behavior. I'm not sure if we exchanged so much as a glance, but somehow Chris (the trainer who picked up my technical mistake described earlier) and I came to a tacit agreement. I would be the good or at least neutral cop and he would be the bad or slightly more confrontational one.

The group was supposed to be describing their ADA training projects. So, I kept asking about the ADA connection. Had the mental health department that she was now trashing violated the ADA? How? Were they covered under the ADA? If so, under which section? What were its obligations? Chris got to be the one to say that it was not okay to wish family members and other members of the community dead because of their disability. I kept bringing her back to the ADA. She calmed down. The rest of the participants went on to share their ADA project ideas.

I had similar positive experiences training as a member of a team. Sometimes we would have two-hour "debriefing" sessions after a training. I confess that this wasn't my favorite thing to do after an eight to ten hour training day, which was to be followed by another eight to ten hour training day. But it made our training better. Sometimes we disagreed with a team member's interpretation of a question or even the law itself. Sometimes we would strategize about ways of reaching participants who for whatever reason weren't getting it. Occasionally, but most important, we gave each other pep talks. It can be easy to get discouraged or overwhelmed when you are spending your third straight weekend in a strange city. Then we would usually go shopping.

Training with partners or as a member of a team is an intimate experience. Co-trainers see you, warts and all, making a fool of yourself in front of lots of people. They read evaluations that fairly and sometimes unfairly evaluate your performance. They know how you respond to stress, confrontation and criticism. They know when you are having an especially bad day. If you work with them often enough they are aware of your quirks and peccadilloes—I used to drink diet soda in a coffee cup during early morning trainings. Potentially even more intimidating, if you were to see it that way, is that they learn this about you purely by training with you without any social contact. Add social contact to the mix and they know that you won't meet with them to work out in the hotel exercise room before a training; that you have considered introducing legislation against early morning meetings of any kind; and that last year you spent both your birthday and Mother's Day on the road and that you are still feeling sorry for yourself because of it.

In short, co-trainers are your new best friends. I've co-trained for love as well as in arranged marriages. As I suspect is the case in arranged marriages, no matter how incompatible you seem initially, with enough compromise and effort you somehow manage to find compatibility. Unlike arranged marriages, training partnerships are time limited. This can help a lot. In the end, I found training with partners infinitely preferable to going it alone.

Rules for Training With Partners Discovered As I Was Training With Partners

1. Get to know the person as well as you can before working together. At minimum, try to sit down with him or her for coffee prior to the training. Obviously, this only works (and then not so well) in scripted trainings, such as legal ones where there is an agreed upon curriculum to be used. It is nearly impossible to improvise with someone that you don't know.

2. Establish ground rules in advance. Decide what you will do if the other person makes an error, doesn't know the answer to a question or otherwise needs assistance.

3. Discuss your respective training styles and how they will mesh. If she takes a more serious approach to training, you might want to tone down or play up your outrageousness. I worked with one trainer who really appreciated my out-there style, but didn't feel

comfortable doing that herself. She encouraged me to be even more strange.

4. Decide how you will deal with your co-presenter running over-time. Do they want you to speak up, hand them a note? Or do they not want to have rigid time requirements at all?

5. Discuss whether or not your co-trainer wants you to sit at the table with him and add your two cents as you see fit or to sit quietly in the back of the room.

TRAINING ACTIVITY: IMAGES

Images is an activity that started out as a core element of my training, but I only do it on occasion now. In Images, I show slides of people with disabilities. The first group of slides are what I call media images of people with disabilities. They range from Tiny Tim in Charles Dickens' *A Christmas Carol* to modern day depictions of people with disabilities used in fund raising. The second group of slides show people with disabilities in everyday life. Unlike the media images, they are active, happy people going about their daily lives.

What I liked about doing Images is that it gave me a chance to talk in depth about the media's depiction of people with disabilities. What I did not like is that some people go to sleep or at least lose interest as soon as the lights go out. Unless it is requested specifically, I usually present a pared down version of Images and try to incorporate a lot of the ideas that arise out of this activity spontaneously into the training.

The crux of the message of Images is that a lot of the negative images that we have of people with disabilities are derived from or at the very least reflected in the media. Although there have been in the last few years more positive images of people with disabilities in the media, negative ones still abound and in some ways are getting worse. I show the March of Dimes poster children whose job it was to raise money to cure polio. To my surprise, these images were not horribly offensive. The postwar message was that we won World War II and now we can win the war against polio. These children looked somewhat sad but they all had their chins up. Then I show images from the Muscular Dystrophy Association's fund raising campaign. These pictures show sad, miserable children at home waiting for the cure. I also display pictures of Jerry Lewis during the annual telethon.

I was nervous when I first started showing images from the MDA telethons and the poster children. Face it, Jerry Lewis and the telethon are sacred cows. Criticizing them is like attacking Mom and apple pie and could potentially alienate an audience. I also didn't want to get distracted by debating with participants the value of telethons. I thought about how to present this for a long time.

I decided to go with factual truth rather than simply my personal opinion, which is of course reflected in the factual truth. At least that's how I see it. I made statements that many people with muscular dystrophy—I don't have MD so that took me out of the fray—feel the telethons are degrading. Some people with MD feel that any benefit derived from the money raised is offset by the damage that is done by portraying competent adults as perpetual children for whom we should all feel sorry. They have nicknamed telethons "pitythons." Depending on how cool the audience is, I tell them that their anti-telethon campaign slogan is "piss on pity." To preserve the credibility of these people with MD, I tell the audience that the former head of the Equal Employment Opportunity Commission, the late Evan Kemp, was one of these individuals with MD who resented being referred to as one of Jerry's Kids, what with being fifty something and the head of a federal civil rights agency and all.

The result has been interesting. Only once has someone questioned a critical perspective on telethons and this was because the participant did not speak English as her native language and didn't understand the point I was making. Other than this, literally no one has questioned the position of people with MD. I guess even sacred cows are vulnerable.

Compared to the extent that the MDA campaign portrays people with disabilities in a negative light, the relatively recent 1995 campaign of the Multiple Sclerosis Society is horrifying. When the campaign was described to me by a friend with MS, I was shocked. When she mailed me a copy of the print campaign I sat and stared at the pictures for a very long time. When I saw the video ad for the campaign, I couldn't speak right away. As you might have guessed by now, it takes a lot to render me speechless even for a short period of time.

So what was the campaign about? You might have seen it. I understand that it was aired until very recently in some cities. The point of the ad campaign is that MS is unpredictable. As someone who for many years didn't know whether she would walk on any given day or use a wheelchair, there is no argument here about the unpredictability of MS. To illustrate this point, the video ad shows a non-disabled looking woman who suddenly, through computer animation, has barbed wire, rope and chain whipped around her eyes and head, reminiscent of a crown of thorns. The narrator says something to the effect that in January, you can't see. Then the barbed wire, rope and chains are whipped around her mouth and the narrator announces that in February, you can't speak. Next, her head and entire torso are covered while the narrator announces that in April, you can't hold your baby, this presumably referring to the baby in diapers at her bare feet.

Aside from wildly hyperbolizing the effects of MS, there are massive problems with this ad campaign. The ads wouldn't make me feel good if I were newly diagnosed with MS. The ads would not encourage me as an employer to hire or promote an individual with MS. In a time where people with disabilities, particularly women, still have to fight to obtain and retain custody of our children, it does not make me feel good as a parent. As a feminist, I'm appalled that images of violence against women are being utilized to raise funds.

As damaging as these negative images can be to the self-esteem of people with disabilities and the public's perception of them, there is another phenomenon that is probably equally damaging. That is the utter lack of images of people with disabilities in the media. Until very recently, we never saw people with disabilities on commercials, in illustrations or in the movies, unless the movie was specifically about a disabled character and then the portrayal was usually of a stereotype. Even now, as this is beginning to change, most of the images that we see are of athletic, well-built white people with disabilities.

That is Images. I used to show positive images of people with disabilities. Now, with the exception of a few disability rights movement slides, I'm more inclined to ask people to share positive images of people that they have seen in the media or, heaven forbid, in real life.

7

You Can't Get There From Here—The Trials and Tribulations of a Disabled Diversity Trainer

Why should you have to hear about my traveling trials and tribulations? What relevance does it have to you as a trainer or as someone who wants to bring diversity to your organization? None, but it fulfills a neurotic need that I have to vent. Seriously, part of training development is the process one takes to get there. I got a lot of training material from weird stuff that happened on the road. Thinking of these uncomfortable, frustrating, sometimes infuriating experiences as potential training material helped me preserve my sanity and dignity on numerous occasions. It is less likely that you are to burst into tears if you are thinking "This may not be funny now, but it will be a great story to tell in a training" or "How can I build an activity around this?"

Not that I'm obsessed about training or anything, but I had come to see my life, at least while I was traveling, as an extension of training. Not only was I collecting material, I was doing research. What techniques, words and attitudes help people who for one reason or another I need to communicate with, get it? I was learning skills about how to get strangers to listen and give me some approximation of what I wanted as I traveled. If I could get them sufficiently past their discomfort to be able to hear me and help me problem solve in a matter of a few moments, then maybe I could use these skills to get participants to do the same.

Sometimes my motives were at least semi-altruistic. Someone might have a question about my disability and did not know how to ask. I experimented with what put people at ease. Most of the time my motives were more practical. For instance, I got a flat tire in my motorized scooter in an airport and the available staff was totally freaked out about me, my scooter, and what had become their problem. If I was going to get home, I had to get them comfortable. It is called survival.

The approach I took with this situation was my standard I-Know-You-And-I-Can-Figure-This-Out-Together. I had to demonstrate to this guy in the airport that he and I together were resourceful and smart enough to figure out how to get me from the airport terminal to my car, which I had left somewhere in the parking lot, without the aid of my scooter. As soon as I said, "I know you can help me figure this out" in a friendly, calm yet assertive way, I saw the wheels begin to turn. "Someone is picking you up, right?" He was out of luck. "No, I drove myself to the airport this morning." "Okay, wait here." I wasn't even nervous that he was going to bolt at this point. He came back with an airport wheelchair and one of those huge pushcarts. He pushed me in the chair and pulled the cart, which he had loaded with my luggage and scooter, and brought it all to my car. I was impressed.

I use this same technique in training. I have absolute unshakable faith in one, the participants' ability to "get it" about disability and two, the participants' ability to problem solve any issues that may arise in working with, serving or interacting with people with disabilities. Remember how I talked about the need to suspend disbelief sometimes? I make sure that participants, as well as airport and hotel staff and other people I might encounter in my travels, understand that problem solving or just plain being able to help doesn't necessarily mean fixing the situation. It might mean helping you find the person who can. It might mean brainstorming. It might mean presenting all of the options even when they are less than ideal. Primarily, I try to communicate my faith in their ability to assist. It is amazing how people will rise to the occasion when you give them permission to be competent. This concludes the Norman Vincent Peale segment of our story...

Other times, my motives for promoting comfort with people with disabilities was somewhere in between altruism and self-interest. See, I'm a chatter. No, I'm not one of those obnoxious people on airplanes who rambles to the poor passenger who happens to be trapped beside them. I'm rather quiet on planes. Really. I have been known to engage in brief small talk with people in lines and hotel lobbies. If strangers are horribly preoccupied with your equipment, they simply won't talk to you. Worse yet, they dart those uncomfortable my-mother-told-me-not-to-stare-at-people-that-are-different-but-I-really-want-to-look-and-besides-not-looking-would-be-rude glances at me. So, I sometimes take it upon myself to help put them at ease.

Is this or should this be the obligation of everyone with a disability who travels or is out and about in the world? Of course not. Should it be my job to do this as someone who has committed the better part of my life to raising awareness about disability and disability issues? The answer that I arrived at after a fair amount of soul searching is: only if and when I want to.

I thought about calling this chapter "Nothing Good Ever Happens at O'Hare." Not that I have anything against Chicago or even the airport itself, but that happens to be the place where I've had many of my most serious mishaps and almost-mishaps while traveling, unless you count hotel fires. This has more to do with Chicago's finicky weather and the sheer size of the airport than the competence of its staff as compared to other airports.

Because of its size, connections are often tight at O'Hare. A wheelchair user has two options as to how her chair might be transported. That is, if the right combination of the following three factors exists: a. the airline is cooperative, b. you know your rights, and c. you have a big mouth.

The first option is to gate check your wheelchair which means that, theoretically, as soon as the plane lands and luggage is unloaded, the airline staff brings you your very own wheelchair. This sounds nice except for a couple of disadvantages. Losing track of the customer and her wheelchair and causing her to miss her connection happens often. Also, it is a largely unknown but indisputable law of physics that if an airline crew is going to damage something stored in the cargo component it will be your wheelchair. I suppose this is better than damaging the family pet, but still…Every time they touch your equipment it is more likely that it will get damaged. Airlines have gotten better about replacing damaged equipment, but that doesn't help you when you are stranded without a chair.

The other option involves leaving your chair in the custody of the airline and letting them worry about transferring it to your connecting plane. The good news is that in my experience they are rather good at getting this to actually happen. The bad news is that they send someone with an airport wheelchair to bring you to your connection. Airport wheelchairs cannot be pushed by the user. They only move when pushed stroller style, although sometimes they can be moved by uppity or desperate people with disabilities who have the lower body strength to pull it off.

In an airport wheelchair you have no control. This wouldn't be a problem assuming that the person pushing your chair is amenable to doing what you ask, speaks English or some other mutual language, and is of the same gender as you if you want to use the bathroom. Probably you do want to use the bathroom since you have another plane to get on and airplane bathrooms are inaccessible. Because I could always walk at least enough to get into the bathroom independently, the gender thing was not that big a deal to me.

The communication thing was. Sometimes the staff has instructions to bring people with disabilities to a designated spot like the Special Passengers Lounge. *Special* is one of those interesting words that has positive connotations for people without disabilities and negative ones for people with disabilities. One poor man was told he had to bring me there. He kept insisting that I wanted to go there. When I asked him why, he explained that they had a television there. They did not have what I desperately wanted, which was an electrical outlet so that I could plug in my laptop. (I had a proposal due the next day.) I convinced him that, although I was sure that the Special Passengers Lounge was a great place, I needed to be near an electrical outlet because I had work to do.

This same man was befuddled that I, as a woman—let alone one using a wheelchair—was traveling by myself. "You are visiting family?" he asked. "No. I'm here on business." "Where is your husband?" "He's home taking care of our son and working at his job." "He lets you travel?" "Yep." Especially when I get to bill for it, I'm thinking. The next question was the one that unnerved me a bit. "Do you ever read the Watch Tower?" That was it. The hairs on the back of my neck were beginning to stand up. I was being pushed through long empty tunnels at O'Hare by a Jehovah's Witness who didn't think that I should be traveling on my own and couldn't understand why I didn't want to go to the Special Passengers Lounge. "No, I can't say that I have read the Watch Tower. So, what's the weather been like in Chicago this summer?" I asked. I'd have asked about the Chicago baseball team had I any idea what its name was. He cooperated in changing the subject. I made my connection and both he and Jehovah left me alone. I didn't need to panic. I think that I even got him to leave me at a place with an electrical outlet. The tough thing about tolerance is that it has to work both ways. Another lesson for me to take with me to the training room…

In all my travels, I never actually got trapped anywhere. I came close once while attempting to come home from Des Moines. I had just finished a fun training series with a great group of people, but after five or so days it's always great to come home. When I got to the airport, it was very crowded. This is a bad sign at a small airport. After I got in line, I noticed that the line wasn't moving—at all. Even after twenty minutes. It turns out that, you guessed it, there was bad weather at O' Hare. Everyone was being rerouted.

My first concern was reaching my husband. At that time he was consulting for a company. So, it wasn't like I could call his secretary and say, "You have to find him." I had the number of the business where he was. So I pleaded with whoever answered the phone to track him down. She started taking me seriously when I explained with just a tinge of hysteria in my voice that I thought I was stranded in Iowa.

My next concern was getting sustenance. This is frequently a concern of mine. The airport restaurant was too crowded to ask serving staff to assist me, so I managed to balance a tray on my lap while I wedged my legs between the carry on luggage that I had crammed onto the floor of my scooter. I found a table with another seasoned traveler—I think I get to call myself that—who mapped out a strategy with me. My goal was to get to Chicago. I had this fantasy that if I got there I would get home the same day.

Not all of my stories of arduous travel involve inaccessible facilities, incompetent airlines or plain old bad weather. Some involve me clumsily trying to utilize my own equipment. For some reason I tended to get new equipment right before an important trip. Okay, they weren't all important trips, but before a trip anyway. Because I don't use a wheelchair or scooter all of the time and because I'm a klutz, I would do well to practice extensively beforehand. Sometimes I think that I have widened more doorways and increased bathroom turning radius through accidents with my electric scooter than I have through advocacy. I once put an eight-inch hole in a store dressing room wall. When I told my companion, she said, "That's what they get for making the dressing rooms so small." I didn't have the heart to tell her that I'd lived in apartments smaller than the dressing room.

In addition to vandalizing property, there was the physical assault component of my travels. I have run over more than my share of feet and toes. The interesting thing is that when you are using a scooter or wheelchair and you run someone over, the assault victim tends to apologize. An assistant of mine once suggested that as a sociology experiment I keep a log of the number of people that apologized who *I* hit.

The most potentially traumatic of these encounters was in Texas when I was backing out of an airport bathroom stall. Since it was a women's room, there was a line—don't get me going on potty parity. Since it was July in Houston, all of the women were wearing open-toed sandals. Since I had a brand new scooter, I was particularly dangerous. The women sensed that I was new or just inept at driving my chair; this probably had more to do with the fact that I kept banging into the toilet on the way out than intuition. They looked frightened as they backed against the wall. I took a deep breath and told them that if everyone watched out for their own toes we all might be okay. They laughed and were really glad to see me leave without amputation or other incident.

Then there is the mechanical aspect of equipment. Equipment breaks, sometimes with alarming frequency. Responsible people with disabilities, especially those who travel, take the time to master the ins and outs of their equipment. Even if they physically can't repair or assemble their equipment because of their disability, they learn how to instruct someone else. They get past their sense of mechanical disinclination and they rise to the occasion. Some carry tools and tire patch kits. Then there is me. I've chosen to rely on the kindness of strangers and the old I-know-we-can-figure-this-out-together routine. The sad part is that it has worked.

It is expected, if not appreciated, that sometimes people in The World will treat you badly because of your disability. If this doesn't happen, it means that you have a charmed life or that you don't go out enough. It's tough when people who you think should know better don't—particularly when they are clients. You know, the people who are telling you to teach them about what they are theoretically doing wrong. It becomes much dicier when their theory clashes with your reality. I think about one instance where I had been working for a year on facilities access as part of a multi-disciplinary team. We went to another of their out-of-state sites to do training on their legal obligations.

They knew that I would be using my chair because I told them in advance. When I got to the site, people looked at me a little funny. I assumed that they were mad at me about some inadvertent faux pas that I had made, because that's what I assume when people look at me funny. I came to realize that the only meeting space in the building was inaccessible. The team, of which I was the only disabled member, left the choice up to me. I could run away screaming. I could allow some of the client's staff to carry me. I could prevail on team members to carry me. I chose the latter.

I didn't make this choice easily, though I made it quickly. For a split second, my inner activist and my inner trainer were in a battle to the death. The inner activist wondered what this meant about the many times that I had done civil disobedience at inaccessible places with less provocation. She wondered if I was selling out. The inner educator reminded her that these people had asked for help and I owed them that much. See, my inner educator is more of a people pleaser than my inner activist. My inner trainer, who like all good trainers is good at facilitating compromise, struck a deal and said that if I allowed myself to be carried in I would get to tell them precisely how and why what they had done was illegal. She also promised to find training material in the experience.

Having been carried into the room and having my lunch brought in rather than be carried out again, I did the training. For a few minutes, while I wondered if anyone would join me for lunch, I was back in high school when the principal asked my mother and me if I would mind eating lunch alone every day because the cafeteria was inaccessible. Except this time people joined me. I did the training, which was intended to be strictly on the ADA but now had awareness elements woven in. It went over well even as I explained that what they had done was illegal. When I got home, my inner educator, inner activist and I made the Crusader mask.

No tales from the road chapter would be complete without a section on hotel fires. I can't say I developed that many training activities from hotel fires, but I did learn a little about human nature. My first hotel fire wasn't an actual fire, but a series of fire alarms. Still, each time the alarm went off we had to evacuate as if it were a fire. Of course, this was the night before the first major training for a project on ADA and public schools. I had two major revelations from this experience. The first was that most people are asleep at midnight. People came out of their rooms and it was clear that they had been asleep, some for a long time. As a life long insomniac I found this curious. I guess that I intellectually knew that many people were asleep at midnight, but witnessing it first hand was a different matter. My second revelation was that most people travel with slippers. Who knew?

The next hotel fire that happened while I was traveling on business (there was another when I was traveling with my family) was a bona fide electrical fire. The alarm went off; this time as I was preparing to go to sleep and it was only about 11:30. I was at a point where I was walking unassisted but my training partner Chris used a wheelchair. As I quickly got to his room, Chris, the ever-mellow Buddhist, was starting to think about getting up and dressed. He was convinced it was a false alarm. Just as he said that, a slightly hysterical voice came over the PA system and announced that this was not a drill and that everyone should evacuate the building immediately. I called downstairs to notify desk staff that Chris and I were waiting on the 19th floor. I opened the door to the stairwell and could smell burning plastic. This seemed to be an electrical fire. Of course, we were calm, at least outwardly. Chris probably was inwardly, as well. It did cross my mind that if push came to shove, I could get down all of those stairs; I wouldn't be able to move for weeks, but so what. I would not, however, be able to get Chris down the stairs.

About twenty minutes later, the fire department came to get us. We were in no actual danger because the fire had been contained and we got to evacuate via the elevator, but we didn't know it at the time. This information would have been useful.

We ended up spending the next several hours on the street waiting for the situation to be resolved. Fortunately, it was a hot June night. At one point, staff from an adjacent hotel came rushing out to bring Chris a blanket. It being about eighty degrees with 100 percent humidity, he politely declined. I guess they'd seen too many movies with the crippled guy with a blanket in his lap. The good news was that they discounted our hotel fee by 50 percent. Our client was paying for our stay, so this wasn't very good news. The bad news is we still had to do a training early the next morning. The other bad news is that I was on the late news in my teddy bear nightshirt. At least I would derive training material from this experience.

The next morning I complimented the staff on how they handled the situation. I compared it positively to my last hotel fire experience. A customer that overheard told me that I traveled too much.

TRAINING ACTIVITY: WHO LIVES WHERE?

I call this activity that I think I made up during a training while participants were working in small groups Who Lives Where? It is simple and provides the opportunity to bring up some powerful issues.

I describe three actual people without using their real names, of course. I describe their disability, how it affects them and I identify gender. June is legally blind and has no other disability. People who are legally blind have impaired vision, but some residual sight. Paul has cerebral palsy that affects his mobility and causes him to use a wheelchair. He is also legally blind. Billy has muscular dystrophy, is thirty-three years old, and cannot sit up. He has used a gurney to get around since he was thirteen. He uses oxygen roughly 80 percent of the time. I explain that one lives in the regular community, one lives in housing just for people with disabilities, and one lives in a nursing home. After this, I challenge participants to guess who lives where.

Take a minute right now and decide what you think before you read on. Have you made your guesses? No cheating.

Depending on the size of the group and the amount of time available, I have participants discuss the question of who lives where in small groups or discuss it with the entire group. Groups are torn about how to answer this. Some are convinced that it's a trick, which it is. Others feel that it couldn't be a trick because one way of answering it is so obviously wrong. After a while, I hear their guesses. Then I tell them the actual right answers.

Here it goes. June, the woman whose only disability is that she is legally blind, lives in a nursing home. The group at this point looks puzzled. "Oh," I say, "I left out one detail. She's eighty-three." They smile after having been let in on the joke. But then I wonder out loud why it is okay for her to be in a nursing home now even though she is physically strong and mentally competent. Sometimes you can get away with wondering things out loud rather than stating them as an opinion. The idea that at least some people who are in nursing homes don't belong there is in some ways a radical one.

Paul lives in congregate housing for people with disabilities. This is not his preference, but it is the only way that he can get even halfway adequate transportation and personal assistance. He is working to change this so that someday he can move back to his hometown.

So far, at this point the audience is still with me. Until they realize what this means about Billy. I explain to them that Billy is the late Reverend William Zeller Robinson. I knew him because he used to be the Board President of the independent living center that I ran. Not only did Billy live independently in the community, he had a wife and two kids and was the pastor of his own church. He did this all from a stretcher. At this point, I posit that if Billy could live in the community, I wonder how many other people that are now in nursing homes could live on their own with proper support should they so choose.

I usually take some time to tell the group a little bit more about Billy and how I came to know him. I didn't take it completely in stride the first time I met Billy and I make a point of telling groups that. The first time I met him was at the opening of the independent living center. About a hundred people came to our open house to find out what we were about and to wish us well. Out of the corner of my eye I saw this big van pull up with *Maranatha Assembly of God* painted on the side. It had the biggest lift on it that I had ever seen. I got distracted and forgot about it. Later, I became aware of this guy in a three-piece suit who used oxygen lying on a stretcher in my new office. I took a deep breath and went over and introduced myself. It turned out that the kids were his, he was a minister, and he never sat up. The membership quickly seized on him and asked him to be a board member. Knowing a good thing when they saw it, they made him board president within six months.

I think it is important for participants to understand that even people with disabilities are sometimes uncomfortable with someone who has a disability with which they are unfamiliar. Even disability rights activists. Even disability diversity trainers. I tell them that at first, Billy's stretcher was very present for me. I was somewhat uncomfortable. This probably had as much to do with him being a minister as it does his disability, but that's another story. This discomfort went away the moment that he made what I thought was a bad decision as board president. Then we were just colleagues who disagreed.

I came to consider Billy to have been one of the finest people with whom I had ever worked. Billy died from complications from an aneurysm in 1991 at age thirty-three, but sometimes I could swear that he's in the room for this activity.

The nice thing about Who Lives Where? is that because I use real live people who I know personally, no one can argue that the individual's living situations would or could never happen as they had. Do more people as disabled as Billy live in institutions than independently in the community? Yes. Are you more likely to live in the community if your only disability is that you are legally blind? Yes, again. But that only strengthens my point that external circumstances play a greater role in determining whether a person with a disability is institutionalized than does their actual disability.

One of the many things that made Billy able to live outside of an institution was strong family connections and commitment. His family of origin saw that he got a good education. They must have had the same high expectations of him that he had of himself as an adult. The other individuals may not have had similar resources.

I sometimes tell a story of three individuals with severe cerebral palsy. Cerebral palsy is a disability that results from damage to the motor nerve of the brain. It can affect one's ability to walk, talk and generally control one's voluntary muscles. Depending on where the brain is damaged, people with cerebral palsy may or may not have mental retardation. What these three individuals have in common was that their parents were told to place them in what was then referred to as a training school. Read hellish institutions where no one learns or is trained to do anything. One of the reasons that their parents were told to forget about these children is that they would never walk, talk or function cognitively above the level of a two-year old. The parents of each of these individuals didn't listen to the experts. Instead, they kept their kids at home and made sure that they got educated. The three kids are adults now. One is the executive director of a non-profit organization. One is a retired director of a state agency. The third is an Ivy League educated attorney.

This is not to say that it would have been more okay to place their children in institutions had they had cognitive impairment, but it does kind of make you wonder about the kids whose parents didn't have the resources and class privilege to question authority. I doubt that they loved their kids any less.

I emphasize to groups that I don't want anyone to think that for one moment I am blaming families who find it necessary to place children, aging parents and other loved ones in nursing homes and other institutions. Lots of times, there are no other alternatives. There is relatively little community support for keeping people with severe disabilities at home. Unless a family has resources such as time and money and bodies to provide care, it can be impossible. This is going to be the case until viable services are provided in the community.

8

Limits of Training

I think or at least hope that the benefits of training are obvious. Most people get something out of it. Some people change their behavior as a result. A few people have major breakthroughs and gain insight into the human condition. People tend to become a little more familiar with and hence less frightened of the unknown whether it is people with disabilities or people of a different race or sexual orientation. For at least some people, this insight sticks. When this happens, organizations change.

I also hope that the limits are obvious. Major organizational and personal change does not happen in a three-hour or three-day training. It takes ongoing training and exposure. It takes a commitment to tolerance. Particularly in the case of disability diversity, it literally represents a different way of doing business.

Organizations tend to see diversity training as a fix, as in: "We've had diversity training, so our behavior couldn't be ableist, or racist, or sexist, or homophobic." This kind of reminds me of neglectful parents who are appalled by their child's anti-social behavior because after all, he was in therapy. The truth is that an organization can't hire a consultant to come in and handle diversity for them. A consultant can teach legal requirements, and in the case of disability, suggest structural modifications and spark awareness of the issue. Promoting and maintaining a diverse environment is much like parenting in that organizations require continuous attention and nurturing to achieve this goal.

The less obvious limitation of disability training and other forms of diversity training is its superficiality. This isn't to suggest that we don't deal with important issues. But we tend to discuss situations that are relatively easy to fix. We look at people who could work with some creative reasonable accommodation or if there was less bias in hiring. We talk about people with disabilities who have been successful despite overwhelming odds. We explore ways that our attitude restrains people with disabilities as well as ourselves. We examine the roles of assumptions, myths, stereotypes and archetypes on people with disabilities.

There is a way in which we don't look at any of the really hard stuff during most trainings. For instance, we don't discuss the people who because of their disability cannot work. There are many fewer than we used to presume but that doesn't mean there aren't any. I'm not talking about the person with mild mental retardation or a severe physical disability, but the man who cannot move or speak and there is not enough cognitive function to determine whether he sees. I'm talking about the person with the psychiatric disability that no one knows how to communicate with. I'm talking about people who were so severely abused in psychiatric institutions (or what in some states are inappropriately called schools) and who are so physically and emotionally injured that any ability or potential they once had has been squelched. What about them?

The bottom line is that we as a society treat people with disabilities horribly. Our society is just beginning to find ways to include people with disabilities who have attributes that we value—namely the ability to generate income—and we're not doing such a hot job at that. But we have no clue how to treat people who are not "productive" or whose behaviors do not conform sufficiently to societal norms.

Americans are peculiar, not so much in how we treat people who are "other," but in the stories that we tell ourselves about how we treat these people. We like to think that we are nice. We can hardly imagine living in "primitive" cultures that expose (read kill) infants. We can't imagine letting aging parents drift off on an iceberg. Yet, we do the moral equivalent all the time.

We used to talk of putting people "away." Most people gave little thought to where exactly "away" was or what it looked like. Often times "away" was an institution. Sometimes it was called a school; other times it was called an asylum. Frequently, it was simply referred to as a "Home." Just about everyone lives in a home or did back then before the homelessness epidemic. But everyone knew the difference between a home with a small *h* and a Home with a big *h*. People bought or moved to homes with small *h*'s. People were placed in ones with big *h*'s. Many of the institutions are closed now with the exception of nursing homes, which somehow don't count because mostly old people live there.

Lip service has been paid to the concept of integrating people with severe disabilities into the community. Many institutions have been closed. Group homes and supported living facilities have been built. They have not delivered on their promise to help people have a full, normalized life. Too many group homes, halfway houses and other assisted living arrangements have become, and often always were, mini-institutions. If you don't believe me, check out the rate of reported abuse that happens in these places. Check out the type of programming that actually happens. We all get reassured when we hear someone is in a program. I used to until I visited some. After I saw adults with Master's degrees coloring restaurant children's menus as part of their program, I began to get jaded. And this was one of the good ones.

These realities—the physical and emotional abuse, sexual assault and less blatant forms of neglect and abandonment that some colleagues I know refer to as "life wasting"—are what I don't know how to address in the context of a training. The truth is, as opinionated as I am, I don't have solutions for lots of these problems. Sure, I can say, "Don't abuse people with disabilities, that's not nice." But what can we do to protect people who are vulnerable and isolated, particularly when the reason they are isolated is that they are just not valued by the society to begin with? Remember, I'm not talking about the people with severe physical disabilities who managed to get a college degree or people with cognitive disabilities who can hold down a job in a fast food restaurant. I'm talking about people who we don't like as a society—people who we don't like because their economic value is not obvious.

I've participated in trainings that grapple with these issues. The only people who are participants are human service providers. Even their willingness to hear these messages is low. You can't blame them. Who wants to hear that the vast majority of services offered in their industry—and we're lying to ourselves if we pretend that it is not an industry—are at best useless and at worst harmful? So, for now, I present the material that people can hear and tell them about ways that they can make a meaningful difference.

9

Bringing Diversity to Your Organization

So, you want to make your company, business, non-profit, city government, state agency, school, or religious organization (did I leave anybody out?) more diverse. How do you go about doing that? I hope that you got some ideas while reading the book so far, but in case you missed something I'm going to spell out some ideas in this chapter.

Who gets to bring diversity to an organization? It helps if you are the CEO or executive director or mayor or someone who has been designated The Boss. Being in charge will certainly make bringing about change easier what with all the power and control. But—and I really want to stress this—it is not required. Yes, you too can help bring about organizational change even if it is not officially in your job title. How do you do this? Well, you might be someone who is what is as known as an opinion leader. An opinion leader is the person with a lot of experience and wisdom who isn't the boss but whom everybody goes to when they want input on a problem. Being an opinion leader is as good if not better than being the boss if you want to implement organizational change.

Leaders in organizations generally don't have that word in their job title. I used to have the idea that you could tell who the leaders were by their job titles. One time I was bidding with a colleague on a job to help with an ADA Self-Evaluation for a city. Bids were to be submitted to the ADA coordinator who was the director of Parks and Recreation. We submitted our bid despite this. To us, having the Parks and Recreation director the designated ADA coordinator indicated that this municipality did not take its ADA obligations very seriously. They probably assumed, as too many cities did, that the ADA only has ramifications for architecture, not policies and procedures that cut across the entire organization. Everybody knows that if they understood the ADA and took it seriously, the ADA coordinator would have been the head of Human Resources or corporation counsel. Yes, I realize that we were guilty of "everybody knows-ing," but we didn't catch ourselves at the time.

You can guess the punch line. Not only was he an appropriate person in the city, he was probably the most appropriate person. Everyone respected him across the board, he was a great leader and he had a particular interest in disability issues. Sometimes being flat out wrong can be so good.

But what if you are not an organizational leader, even informally? As I said, it will be harder, but you can still bring about some modicum of change. For one thing, you can always educate. I remember doing a training in a small company where literally everyone from the president to the janitorial staff attended. One of the janitors told a really poignant story about his wife being at the mall with their severely disabled daughter and being told by another shopper that she should not take a child like that out in public. People in the room were appropriately outraged. Then they started asking the janitor questions about services for his child and educational opportunities and about his daughter's rights in general. My guess is that he wasn't often in the role of trainer in staff meetings. But, it was clear to everyone in the room that he had more expertise than anyone else.

I don't mean to imply that every person in every organization can cause major or even minor change in his or her company or that it is solely your responsibility. Face it, there are some organizations, for profit and non-profit alike, which are rather dense or uneducated. Some just don't care. What I am saying is that you might be able to facilitate more change than you think and you should give it a try if it's important to you.

So here are a few things that you might do to promote disability and other types of diversity in your organization. We've already established that all audiences are alike. Differences in style, appearance and social cues are mere window dressing. Organizations where people work, go to school or otherwise participate in may be structurally, economically and politically different and may serve different purposes, but they are made up of people who are fundamentally alike. So, I don't want any of you saying to yourselves as you read this that these ideas could never be applied to MY business, social service agency, hospital, city government, school, college, corporation, church, synagogue, because MY organization is too conservative, liberal, big, small, rich, poor, etc. That can be a cop out. If a technique really doesn't fit within your organizational culture, I challenge you to find a way to adapt it so that it becomes compatible.

Things Individuals and Organizations Can Do to Promote Diversity

Hire a Trainer

Hire a trainer, preferably for numerous sessions. There, was that self-serving enough? Seriously, it's not a bad idea to have an outsider come into an organization to bring a message that you and some others may already know and are able to provide. I was once asked to do some ADA training for a municipality. The ADA coordinator was in this case a great trainer who had an excellent command of the material herself. I asked why she was willing to pay me out of her paltry budget to come in and present material that she knew. She said, "That's simple. They'll listen to you in a way that they never would me." I find that this happens a lot, though certainly not all of the time. It's not so much that familiarity breeds contempt as it breeds complacency.

Notice that I said hire a trainer, as in *pay them*, not as in *recruit a volunteer*. You want a trainer that knows what he or she is doing. Carefully check out their credentials, experience level and references. This is particularly true if you are going to allow a trainer to utter a word about the law in the presence of people that are part of your organization. We don't all know what we are doing and often you get what you pay for.

Sometimes, because someone has a disability, a couple of things are assumed. The first is that the person is educated in and articulate about disability rights and disability diversity issues. The second assumption is, because an individual has a disability, he or she is educated about other disabilities. These two assumptions are usually only true for the minority of us who choose to promote disability rights as our lifework.

Particularly in the area of disability, people expect you to be able to train for free (though my friends who specialize in other areas of diversity report this as well). There is also an assumption that we are funded by grants to provide our services or we all live on benefits. Worse yet, the issue of compensating us for our services is not considered at all. I hate to say this, but in my experience, it is most often fellow non-profit organizations that make this assumption. After all, they reason, they are strapped financially, which is almost always the case, and they are fighting the good fight, which is usually the case. While having worked for many starving non-profits, I certainly empathize, it is important to recognize that diversity trainers have to feed their families, too. The primary way that we demonstrate that expertise is both legitimate and valuable is to pay money for it. Or as one friend of mine said after I told a non-profit that I would have to charge for my services and they responded by saying but they were a non-profit organization, "I wonder if they tell that to the electric company."

The right trainer can diffuse organizational tensions about diversity, bring fresh insight to a situation and assist in problem solving. Plus, if the individual has a disability—I recommend that he or she does—or trains with someone who has a disability, she or he can help start to demystify "the disabled" and disability.

Get As Clear As You Can About the Issue

Whether the issue is race, gender, sexual orientation or disability, an important step that you can take is to get as clear as you can about the issue. Whether you're the CEO or a secretary, you, as the one who wants to initiate change, are a role model about understanding the issue because you are the one interested in promoting it. The better that you understand the problem, the more convincing you'll be in persuading others that the problem exists, should be taken seriously and maybe even is fixable. The process of getting clear about the issues will look different to different people depending on individual style, personality and maybe even position within the organization.

Some people may want to read everything about the issue that they can get their hands on; others may want to talk to "experts"; other people may want to talk to people who aren't white, who are gay, or who have disabilities. Still others won't want or need to do any of this type of research. They will just need to be deeply aware that there is a problem, whether it is inaccessible architecture or a less than welcoming environment, and that it needs to be addressed. For them, establishing moral certainty is crucial in gaining credibility. None of these approaches is necessarily more valid than the next. Do what you need to do to establish internal and external credibility.

Accept that as a member of this society you are ableist or racist or whatever the *ist* in question is. Acknowledge it. Work on changing it. Whatever you do, don't beat yourself up about it. It is counterproductive and boring. Besides, guilty people are probably the second hardest group of people to train. The first hardest are people who think that they already know it. The more of your own stuff that you can work through, the more effective you will be at facilitating change.

Assess the Environment

No, this doesn't mean that you have to be able to conduct a full-scale architectural accessibility survey before you can make your organization diverse. It does mean that on some level you should check out the physical and non-physical environment. The truth is, without some training, you are for the most part not going to be able to conduct an accurate accessibility survey. Just because a bathroom has a grab bar doesn't make it accessible. However, you will be able to notice things like steps or the absence of a TTY (a telecommunication device used by people who are deaf or who have speech disabilities that enables them to communicate by phone). I'm not saying that you have a legal obligation to fix these barriers; you may not. I'm just inviting you to make a note of them.

Assess the non-physical environment as well. You know by now that as a person without a disability you will never be able to simulate the experience of having a disability any more than you could being of another race. However, it's not bad to attempt to look at your organization through the imaginary eyes of somebody with a disability. Are there workers with disabilities? Are there customers with disabilities? If someone with a disability were to look at your organization's catalogue, advertising or other print materials would they see anyone else with a disability? Would a TTY number be included in this material?

Accessible features in the environment are more than just amenities to people with disabilities. They make the difference between being able to utilize a facility and participate in an organization or not. Images of people with disabilities in advertising and other materials are an affirmation of an organization's commitment to be inclusive. Depicting people with disabilities combats invisibility.

How would somebody with a disability be treated in your organization? It might be hard to evaluate this if not too many people with disabilities spend time there. Questions that might be helpful are: *How does the organization regard people and ideas that are different? Is difference embraced or avoided?* If your organization is like most, the truth probably lies somewhere in the middle. The answers to these questions, as well as the results of your assessment, should give you some insight into ways to begin making your organization more welcoming to people with disabilities.

Tune Up Your Organization's Problem Solving Skills

People who are comfortable solving problems are more comfortable with, and hence more welcoming of, people with disabilities. In organizations, much of the negative experiences of people with disabilities happen because someone on staff lacked problem solving skills. When people don't know how to solve problems, they get scared. When they get scared, they act inappropriately.

Take, for example, the telephone receptionist who repeatedly hung up on someone with a speech disability. This actually happened. When confronted, she said that in twenty years of doing this job she had never had to deal with someone like that and she wasn't about to start now. When probed a little, it was easy to see that this woman was scared out of her mind and had no idea what to do. If her organization had more of a problem solving orientation, she might have figured out a way to distinguish what the caller was saying or located someone else who could. Locating someone else with the ability to problem solve is key. It is simply not reasonable to expect that every staff member will be able to solve every disability-related problem. It is reasonable to expect that every staff member will be able to direct someone with a problem that they can't solve to a designated individual. Assigning a staff member to problem solve disability issues will reduce the panic a staff member feels when confronted with someone whose speech they can't understand. The stress reduction alone may enable the staff person to solve problems more independently.

The receptionist story brings up a critical point about training. Should your organization opt for diversity/awareness training, include line staff. I can't tell you how many times corporations, non-profits, and businesses have asked me to provide training to senior management but not line staff—the people who actually interact with the public on a day-to-day basis. I remind them that if the people who answer the phone or sit at the counter don't deal well with people with disabilities, it doesn't matter what policies they have developed or how diversity is reflected in their mission statement. These first contact people are truly the ones who can make or break an organization's diversity efforts.

In case you hadn't already noticed, problem solving skills, as well as other ways of creating a welcoming environment for people with disabilities, generally foster better relationships with customers and staff. The better your customer service is, the better employees will deal with the needs of people with disabilities and vice versa.

Have People in the Organization Learn Disability 101

This suggestion flows from the one to hire a trainer. Its basic premise is that knowledge is a good thing. It can help diffuse tensions and misconceptions about people with disabilities that may have arisen in your organization. Negative ideas, such as ADA mandates that people with disabilities be given special treatment, are easily diffused with a little education. If you can, expose employees to rudimentary legal requirements and some other disability basics. In my experience, very few people stay resistant to including people with disabilities when they find out what the legal requirements actually are and what it is that most people with disabilities want and expect in terms of treatment.

Be Prepared to Fire Someone with a Disability

If you're not willing to fire someone with a disability, then you have no business hiring him or her in the first place. Since it is illegal for many organizations not to hire a qualified person with a disability, we all should get comfortable disciplining and, when necessary, firing people with disabilities.

Not only do you have to get to a place where you discipline and fire people with disabilities as you would any other employee, you need to get to the point where you treat them as you would anyone else all the time. This means getting angry as well as being demanding, rude and generally snotty, assuming that is the way that you treat other employees. If it is not, good for you and don't treat people with disabilities like that, either.

What I'm getting at is—Cliché Warning—it is vital to be able to see the person rather than the disability. What they often leave out in the cliché is that when you stop seeing the disability and start seeing the person you will see a person with flaws, kind of like everyone else. People act a little stunned in trainings when I whisper that you don't have to like all people with disabilities. In fact, you probably shouldn't, because we're not all nice. But it is the truth. Nothing squelches inclusion of people with disabilities in an organization like the pressure to like everyone in a certain group.

I obviously deal with lots of instances where organizations are reluctant to hire and promote people with disabilities. If this didn't happen a lot, I'd be out of a job and the unemployment rate of people with disabilities wouldn't be approximately 75 percent. Employment discrimination certainly isn't the only reason that people with disabilities are unemployed. But I sometimes encounter situations in organizations where the opposite is true. People who happen to have disabilities are hired and promoted or retained when they are not qualified. It is one of the secrets we don't like to talk a lot about in the disability rights movement. Here are a couple of real life scenarios.

Applicant X applies for a job. Interviewers are so impressed that she can live alone and "get around like that in her wheelchair" that they assume she must be qualified to do the job and don't probe as rigorously as they normally would during the interview. Plus, they were a little nervous around her…

Employee Y has been a good employee for twenty years. He has never caused any trouble and just about everybody likes him. He gradually acquires a visual disability. He is no longer able to perform his job as a safety inspector. His supervisor and coworkers know this but look the other way and try to compensate as best they can...

These kinds of situations are less common than ones in which the applicant is not hired despite her superior qualifications, or an employee with a newly acquired disability is let go because it is inaccurately perceived that he can no longer do his job, but they do occur. Sometimes, it is harder to get organizational staff to understand that hiring, retaining and promoting unqualified people with disabilities is as big a problem, if not bigger than not hiring, promoting or retaining employees with disabilities.

Granted, it doesn't present the same legal issues, but it does present a host of other problems. First of all, it can hurt employee morale. No matter how well-liked someone is, no matter how impressed co-workers are by a person's ability to confront obstacles of day-to-day life, eventually someone will rightfully get resentful. Resentment tends to grow and spread and can quickly permeate an entire department or division. In addition, these practices reinforce the idea that people with disabilities are less competent. It is unfair to the people with disabilities that the organization is ostensibly trying to help out. Maybe the unqualified applicant who was hired and is presumably now making a mess of the job would be a stellar employee in the appropriate position. Maybe the man who can no longer be a safety inspector because of his vision can train others or assume another role in the corporation where he is once again a valued employee. The bottom line is that this type of organizational behavior is patronizing and, no matter how well meaning, is ultimately destructive to people with disabilities as well as to organizations.

Understand That It Is Okay to Make Mistakes

In your quest to include people with disabilities or other groups of individuals previously excluded, you'll probably make some mistakes, kind of like you do with other things. This is all right. If you've blown something, acknowledge it, apologize if necessary and then fix it as best you can.

Forgive Yourself for Not Having Handled It Already

Guilt immobilizes individuals and organizations. Get rid of it now. Lots of times, people and the organizations that they work in are so guilty about what they may have done wrong that they are unable to do an honest assessment of their environment. They are so concerned about their mistakes that they resist and sometimes even refuse to evaluate the organization. Some organizations are hesitant to learn what their legal obligations are for fear of finding out that they are in violation. Sticking your organizational head in the sand never works. What I tell clients who have missed ADA deadlines or have not adhered to internal plans is that they can only begin now. They can't erase the past. They should accept this and move on. Basically, what I am telling them and you is to lighten up already. Get over yourselves and begin to do something.

About the Author

Melissa Marshall is an attorney who graduated from the University of Connecticut School of Law and from Hampshire College in Amherst. She is a person with a disability who lives in West Hartford, Connecticut with her husband Ken and their two sons, Nick and Liam, ages twelve and two.

0-595-21253-0

www.ingramcontent.com/pod-product-compliance
Lightning Source LLC
Chambersburg PA
CBHW020239290526
45784CB00003B/1043